CW01371894

EUSTACE MULLINS

CONVERSATIONS WITH JOHN F. KENNEDY

*Ø*MNIA VERITAS

EUSTACE CLARENCE MULLINS
(1923-2010)

CONVERSATIONS WITH
JOHN F. KENNEDY

The Revelation of Life and Death as transcribed from the record of conversations with the late John F. Kennedy by H.P. MEADE (EUSTACE MULLINS)

PUBLISHED BY
OMNIA VERITAS LTD

*Ø*MNIA VERITAS

www.omnia-veritas.com

FOREWORD	7
CONVERSATION ONE	10
CONVERSATION TWO	55
CONVERSATION THREE	97

FOREWORD

During the spring of 1966, the vision of the late John F. Kennedy, the martyred President of the United States, appeared to me on three separate occasions, in three different places, and engaged me in lengthy disquisitions about the condition of man, the dangers apparent in his present estate, and what must be done to avert them.

I made it clear during these conversations that I was very dubious about the value of anything that I might be able to do, but John F. Kennedy assured me that for a number of reasons, which he explained, I was the likeliest person to proceed with this assignment.

I have lost none of the doubts which assailed me during these conversations. If anything, they have increased. First of all, I can offer no evidence to a mechanist or materialist society that the conversations took place. They must start or fall according to the information which they contain. There are no signed documents; there is no blurred photograph of an evanescent mist which

I could claim to be the spirit of John F. Kennedy returning to his present mode of being. I cannot even say that I actually SAW John F. Kennedy during these conversations.

The physical, or rather, non-physical, circumstances of these encounters were quite simple. On each occasion, I was engulfed by a strange radiance in which the physical world disappeared, and I was serenely aware that I was in the Presence of John F. Kennedy. There was absolute peace, and I was under the impression that nothing ever had or ever could disturb us in these surroundings. It was as though one had attained a state of ultimate beauty, and had left behind forever all the cares of earth.

Although I was under the impression that we were conversing by voice, John F. Kennedy assure me during the conversations that we were not. In retrospect, I can see that ordinary voice would not have been possible, as there was nothing physical in the surroundings in which I could gladly undergo as many times as necessary, and one which I will never forget. Whether it could be described as the next station of life after death, a state of beatifications of these things. I do know from these encounters that John F. Kennedy is now existing in a state of bliss, even though, as he pointed out, he may have to return to earth for another sojourn.

It is the duty of mankind to weigh with the greatest care the admonitions contained in these conversations, and the purpose for which they were made. They may be the greatest contribution of one who during this lifetime offered great opportunities to humanity, and who now, from another sphere, may do more for mankind than he was able to achieve for them while on earth.

CONVERSATION ONE

Early in 1966, I began to be troubled by the persistence of some force outside of myself. This force, at the same time, seemed to be within myself. I found it difficult to concentrate on anything, and it became more and more trying to accomplish my daily tasks. I seriously began to consider enlisting the aid of a psychiatrist, although I realized that I had little to tell him except a sensation of vague disquiet. I knew that I was physically well; I had no pains or symptoms of any organic disorder, and had long enjoyed the state of being which is known as "perfect health".

Nevertheless, as soon as I thought of consulting a psychiatrist, this troublesome force warned me that it would be a mistake. I was not to speak of this problem to anyone until I had faced it at its sources, that is, until I had come to terms with the strange, disturbing presence.

Although I realized that the choice had been opened to me, I continued to postpone making it. The result was a succession of sleepless nights, and days of preoccupation during which the presence interfered with my work. I became aware that I could not ignore this presence much longer. Despite the fact that I was getting hardly any sleep, and that I was unable to relax at any time, my health was not at all affected. I remained free from any ailment or any problem of a physical nature. Even though I knew that I could put an end to my predicament at any time by allowing myself to face this presence, I was still reluctant to do so, because I knew instinctively that one I did so, life would never again be the same for me.

This was hardly a logical reaction on my part, as matters could hardly be worse for me. Excepting the fact that I enjoyed good health, there was little else which I might fear to lose. I had no money or property, and I worked at a difficult job which hardly paid my expenses, so that any change would be for the better. I was an insurance inspector, and my work demanded considerable travel on unpaved roads in remote areas of the counties, but the fees in many cases did not cover my expenses. There were many weeks when the cost of maintaining my automobile exceeded my income. Because of the accuracy of my reports, the work had steadily increased during a two-year period, but my expenses continued to take most of the income. The insurance companies had learned that an inspector was available who would make longer trips for no extra fee, and of course they were delighted. It was a discouraging occupation, but because of the widespread unemployment in our area, there was nothing else I could find to do, and my income continued to be less than that of welfare recipients in our large cities.

During one such trip, on a rough, dusty road several miles west of Lyndhurst, Virginia, I suddenly felt an overpowering weariness. This was unusual, as I was often on the road twelve or fourteen hours a day, but I rarely became tired. On this occasion, it seemed impossible for me to go on, and I pulled the car over to the side of the road, coming to rest in a little clearing. I remember the right-hand fender brushing against the leaves of a tree, and then I was into another world.

My first impression was that of light, continuous and all-embracing light. It was as though I were placed in the middle of a diamond, or sitting in the source of all light. I remained passive, letting this light play through me, and after some time or a period of waiting, I realized that I was not alone. In the light with me was the strange, disturbing presence which had annoyed me for so long. I was able to look at it, and I felt a great surge of relief that at last, whether for good or evil, I would know what was facing me. Again, time passed, how long I could not say, but the presence seemed warm familiar. I slowly began to understand that I was in the Presence of John F. Kennedy.

"You look rather foolish", said JFK.

"I feel foolish", I said. "You seem so real."

"Of course I'm real", he said.

"But…"

"But I'm dead. Is that it?"

"Well, I do read the newspapers."

"That's precisely why I want to talk to you. I want to explain about death."

"Now that I'm about to hear the answer", I said, "I'm not so sure that I want to. Like everyone else on earth, I have wondered about it."

"You may have wondered about it", said JFK, "but you never really asked yourself about it, did you?"

"Perhaps not."

"I know that you have not. I can remember that much very well from my earthly existence, the refusal of man to ask himself the only two questions which matter."

"What are the two questions?"

"The questions", said JFK, are — Why am I alive? And Why must I die?"

"And you don't thing I have ever asked myself those questions?"

"I know that you have not."

"Is that because I was afraid of the answers?"

"Not really. It was merely that you were not ready for the answers."

"Is that why our religions don't answer them?"

"Like most people on earth, you have a mistaken view of the role of religions. The purpose of religion is to assure you that a way exists, and perhaps to show you the way, but the rest is up to you. Religion cannot be a substitute for life. It is only one aspect of life."

"But why me?" I asked. "Why should you pick me out to hear all this? Am I dead now?"

"No, you aren't dead", said JFK. "In fact, it is now important that you live, as you have been chosen to tell people of earth what I wish them to know."

"I hope you won't get impatient with me and all my Whys, but why are you able to do this? Billions of people have died, but no one has ever been able to explain the mystery of death to those who remained behind."

"The answer to that", said JFK, "is violence. Violence interrupted my destiny. You see, I was intended to bring a new experience of peace to the world. I had been chosen, quite involuntarily, of course, to give mankind some respite from the terrible disasters which have plagued him in recent years. However, my choice was an unfortunate one. There were many serious conflicts in my destiny, which had been intended, as nothing can come into being without some sort of conflict or opposition, but these conflicts proved to be too powerful."

"That's difficult for me to understand", I said. "There are plenty of things which exist without opposition."

"You may think so, if you rely on the naked eye", said JFK, "but if you are aware of the forces of gravity, as well as the much more powerful forces of creation, you would discover that this is not the case. Everything physical comes out of a sort of crucible — it is forged, so to speak. In my case, the conflicting elements which created me were too strong, and instead of carrying out my mission, I was physically assassinated."

"You seem to have survived rather well", I said.

"Bullets cannot affect the soul", said JFK. "The only thing which affects the soul is what we do with our lives. Since I was cut off through no fault of my own, I have been given the opportunity of carrying on my work though an earthly agent."

"Does this happen very often?" I asked.

"No, it is very unusual", he said. "Most people do fulfill their earthly purpose, in one way or another, so that when they come to die they have carried out their earthly tasks, and there is nothing really important which is left undone. In cases such as mine, where the violence had proved too unmanageable, and I had made no preparations to go, I had the choice of remaining on earth as a spirit, or of finding a man who could act as my agent."

"By spirit, do you mean a ghost?" I asked.

"You could call it that", said JFK, "although the term of ghost has been used to cover a number of differing situations. For instance, after departure, as we may conveniently refer to death, it often happens that a soul has to remain in the earthly sphere for some time, for varying reasons, which I won't go into just now. This time may be, in earth time, a few minutes or thousands of years. During this time, these souls are occasionally manifested to some humans, again for varying reasons."

"Then I'm talking to your ghost?" I asked.

"No, indeed", said JFK. "You are talking to the real me. I'm not a ghost, and I'm not imprisoned in the earthly sphere."

"Then where are we now?" I asked.

"That's another difficult question", said JFK. "You see, we don't have any maps here. As a matter of fact, you are still parked two miles west of Lyndhurst, Va., and I am — well, I am where I am."

"And just what is it you wish me to do?"

"Your task is a very simple one. You merely have to write down what I am to tell you, and then you must distribute it on earth."

"That sounds simple enough, but I happen to know it won't be."

"I didn't say it would be a simple task. You'll manage, somehow."

"I'll manage to get myself locked up. That's about as far as I'll get."

"It will be done", said JFK. "I'm not saying you won't have problems, or that you'll be able to do it right away, but it will be done, because it has to be done."

"I can feel that, the urgency of it", I said, "but I still have a question as to why I should be the one to do this — to talk to you, as well as to acquaint the people of earth with these talks."

"That also is simple. You weren't surprised to be here with me, were you?"

"Not really. Perhaps I thought it was another case of Mark Twain, that the reports of your death were greatly exaggerated."

"They always are", said JFK. "You can see me now and talk to me because you have spent many years preparing yourself for just such an encounter."

"I have done a lot of studying and travelling", I said. "I've asked a lot of questions, but very few of them have been answered. Does that qualify me for this?"

"Whether you realized it or not", said JFK, "you have put yourself through a long period of austerity, somewhat like a monk who has shut himself away from most of the things which the rest of the world believes is necessary in their lives. You have raised many questions, and you have neither answered them yourself nor have you accepted what you thought, and which actually were, inadequate answers."

"By inadequate answers, do you mean that I haven't accepted the answers which are offered by the various religious groups?" I asked.

"That's about it", said JFK.

"But I am a believer in Jesus Christ", I told him.

"I'm aware of that", he said. In fact, that is another reason why you were chosen."

"Do you mean that the Christian religion is the answer?"

"As I said before, no religion is the answer", said JFK. "I intend to explain how salvation is a problem of the individual, and how nothing else can do it for him. I pointed out that religion cannot be a substitute for life. It I a question, not an answer. The question, of course, is a multiple one. Can I find salvation? Is death final? And many other questions. Even if one accepts the tenets of any one of the various religious groups, one should realize that these tenets in many cases say what the audience wants to hear. They are tailored to the littleness of man, and in most cases, they ignore the vastness of the universe. Man can hardly go beyond himself by accepting something which allows him to remain as little as he was before. The existing religious systems on earth, as you probably know, originated in the quests of individuals who sought the answers to life and death, Zoroaster, Christ, Buddha, Confucius, Mohammed, they were all seekers after truth. The important thing to remember about them is that each of them was able to remain true to himself while seeking the answers to man's existence. It is for that reason that each of them brought into being a religious system. Nothing worthwhile can be accomplished on earth unless one remains true to one's self."

"If each of these individuals was successful in remaining true to himself, does that mean that mean that each of these systems is equally true?" I asked.

"Now you are exhibiting the most common human shortcoming", said JFK, "the determination to define something by measuring it against something else. You wish to define A by saying that it is larger or smaller than B, or that it is a certain distance from C, but these facts really tell us nothing about A. nevertheless, most human definitions are based on just such criteria.

In regard to the equivalent value of religious systems, I have already said that they evolved from the quests of individuals who managed to find some answers to the riddle of the universe. One of the fundamental values of life on earth is variety. Obviously, the results of the quests of these individuals were not of equal value."

"Do you mean that some of them are more valuable than others?" I asked.

"No, their value lies more in theirs differences", said JFK. "Because variety is one of the values of earth, things which are different have more value than things which are alike."

"You seem to be defining difference as a positive good", I said. "Does that mean that things which are exactly alike are bad?"

"In the constantly evolving economy of the universe", said JFK, "things lose some of their value each time they are repeated."

"But if things that are alike have lesser values", I said, "that sounds as if our industrial civilization is not so good."

"You have probably discovered that shirts which are made to fit everybody don't fit anybody", said JFK. "This doesn't mean that these shirts are evil, it simply means that, in the terms of universal economy, they are useless, or wasted. Also, things which are mass produced have no values of the individual maker in them. It is these values which produce the worthwhile things of life. Rembrandts can bring a million dollars at auction because every home in America doesn't have a Rembrandt on the wall. However, these paintings did not become valuable because of their scarcity, but because of the values which were put into them by their maker."

"I can see that I'm not going to pin you down as to the comparative value of religions", I said. "But, to return to my question, why have you picked me out to hear all this? Wouldn't it have been more logical to approach some member of your family?"

"More logical to you, perhaps, but not to me", said JFK. "It would be very disturbing to any member of my family if I appeared to them. Do you think they would be able to sit quietly and converse as we are doing? It would be a long and tortuous process before any good results could be achieved, if it were possible at all. Then the public would be skeptical of any such conversations, supposing that a family member was simply trying to continue my earthly work in my name. It would be unfair to my family, because death defines a person once and for all, and a reappearance in the same form would cast severe doubts on the reality of the person they knew. That is why those who have passed on appear only briefly, if at all, to those who are left behind, and why they do not enter into any extended relationships with them, such as we are doing now."

"You mean a conversation", I said.

"That is your term for it", answered JFK, "but as a matter of fact, we are not really talking to each other. We are merely expressing thoughts in silence which we receive and respond to."

"Then everything is different here", I said.

"There you go again", said JFK. "Different, yes, but only as death is different from life."

"Now you are getting back to the original intent of this conversation", I said. "You were to explain death to me, and through me, to the people of earth."

"That is one purpose, yes", said JFK.

"Do you mean there is more to it than that?" I asked.

"There is more to everything than that", said JFK.

"Shall we make a beginning, then", I said, "by your explaining the meaning of death to me?"

"Certainly", said JFK. "Life and death are like a playing card which has a design on each side. On one side, or face, is the value which we call life. On the other side, or back, is the design which we call death. During life, we see the face, and death merely turns the card over, so that we see the back. The grief of the survivors is due to the fact that a known face, or value, has been taken from them."

"The faces have different values", I said. "And the backs of the cards carry similar designs. Does that mean that everyone becomes alike in death?"

"From the viewpoint of life, yes", said JFK, "although you must remember that I am putting this as simply as possible."

"And does the departure of a life create a vacancy on earth?" I asked.

"Of course not", answered JFK. "One cannot add to or subtract from the sum total of life or death, or from the values contained therein. In the economy of the universe, nothing is lost or wasted. Energy which has completed its work on one plane immediately goes to work on another plane. Also, many of the values of a departed one survive in those who perpetuate his memory?"

"Are you speaking of a public figure like yourself, or of everyone?" I asked.

"Everyone", replied JFK, "who has lived, leaves something of himself behind on earth. Children, a life's work, both tangible and intangible things, whatever he has managed to accomplish remains for a time. However, this is usually misunderstood by those who survive him, and men are often remembered for the wrong reasons. This is because life itself is a very limited form of consciousness, and those who are alive are largely insensible to the values of life."

"That is a disturbing idea", I said.

"It's not a very new one", said JFK, "and it shouldn't surprise you. No doubt you are familiar with the tests which prove that the average person uses only about ten per cent of his brain power, and even so-called intellectuals use about half of their mental resources. This refers to the energizing aspects of thought, rather than to the phenomenon of consciousness itself, but this concept may aid you in understanding that few people in earth are really conscious. You may remember that the function of the prophets has always been to awaken the people, either to danger, or to the values of life, or whatever. In every case, they began with the premise that the people were asleep."

"Are you trying to say that death is a higher form of consciousness?" I asked.

"Now we are getting back to those comparisons again", said JFK. "In the first place, a dead person is not conscious at all, in the physical sense. He has transcended physical consciousness, and unconsciousness as well. You could say that in some aspects it is a heightened form of awareness, however. For instance, we are conversing without really talking to each other, which would not be possible on a physical plane. The simplest explanation is that it is a non-consciousness, because one is no longer responsive to physical stimuli, or subjected to physical laws. The personal objection to death is a purely physical one, the resentment of the earthly shell that it is being discarded. The soul enters and departs from the earthly shell without difficulty, except when the earthly shell desires to hold onto it for selfish reasons. This is the struggle which usually takes place at the time of death, and it can be an impressive one, as well as one of considerable physical discomfort. However, I was trying to explain the nature of conscious life, and its physical limitations. Because human consciousness has come more and more to depend upon physical stimuli, to the exclusion of everything else, and upon the protection and feeding of the physical shell, most conscious impressions are devoted to that end, and other conscious impressions, of which there are many, which have no direct physical value, are ignored."

"Is that why spirits are so often ignored?" I asked.

"Yes", said JFK. "The manifestation of the spirit of a departed one usually has no direct physical inspiration, since the parted is no concerned with physical things. For that very reason, the conscious humans pay no attention to them. You may be able to understand why spirits, or ghosts, if you will, sometimes get very annoyed, and even violent."

"It's the old problem of communication" I said. "And, speaking of problems of communication, do you really have any idea that I'm going to be able to report this conversation, or that anyone will pay attention to it?"

"Conversations", JFK corrected me. "The only way we can develop this thing satisfactorily is to have a number of meetings, and to allow the impressions which I am giving you to grow to and shape themselves into a suitable earth form."

"I can see the appropriate form right now", I said. "It's a straitjacket, and I'm going to be in it."

"It won't be that bad", said JFK. "You must do everything possible to avoid it, which means that you almost always try to be convincingly sane."

"An attorney once told me that the only people he was dubious about as far as their mental condition was concerned, was when they appeared to be extremely convincing and sane."

"That's often true", said JFK. "In any case, you must avoid being provoked into any outburst which will cast doubts on the validity of the conversations, and I am sure such provocation will be forthcoming. The physical body's first reaction is to defend itself against a conscious impression which it cannot readily assimilate or understand, and this means, in most instances, that it will attack. Conversation is not a natural animal trait, and even the most conscious animals will reject the idea of conversing with a departed one. I might mention that I've had considerable difficulty in reaching you, even though I've been trying for some time. Until now, I always met with complete rejection."

"I was only aware of something which was extremely annoying", I said. "It would have helped if you could have announced yourself."

"That wasn't possible", said JFK, "because I was not allowed to manifest myself on the physical plane. The only way that we could converse was to bring you into my plane."

"That sounds as though I am dead", I said.

"No", replied JFK, "you could be said to be in a "better" world, although there again is the problem of comparisons. My problem in reaching you is that any conscious impressions which does not have a direct physical importance is instinctively rejected by the animal nature. I finally arranged to reach you by inducing in you a state of extreme fatigue. Your animal nature lowered its guard for a moment, and here we are."

"Here indeed", I said. "I wish I knew where "here" is."

"Here is just where it always has been and always will be", said JFK. "But I must explain to you in greater detail the nature of human consciousness, and why it has made these conversations necessary. You may know that the human embryo, while it is still in the mother's womb, begins to establish and receive impressions of warmth and vibration, and even sound. However, it is still in darkness. Only after birth does the child become aware of light, and as it grows, it increases its power of receiving impressions rapidly during the first few years of life. As these impressions become adequate for sustaining its life, the human gradually limits or cuts back its power of receiving impressions, although, if they continued to grow at the rate which they maintain during the first few years of life, humans would be able to speak without using speech, just as we are doing now."

"Do you mean that the consciousness of an adult is as limited as that of a child?" I asked.

"I mean that it is the same thing", replied JFK. "There are no humans who have fully developed their powers of impression through the years of maturity. The reason is a simple one. As the child becomes older, he learns to establish correct impressions of most of the things necessary for his well-being. However, the powers of impression go far beyond this. For instance, you have often been aware of someone else's opinion of you, even though nothing has been said."

"That's true", I admitted.

"And you have been often aware of what another person was thinking, perhaps during a conversation, and that what was being said was quite different from what that person was thinking about the topic of discussion."

"That does happen", I said.

"So that your powers of impressions, in going beyond the conversation or your dealings with others, open the door to many sorts of unpleasantness, or they pose many problems which, if you avoided these extra impressions, could have been avoided. As this sort of thing happens frequently to those whose powers of impressions have become more developer, what is the natural result?"

"They try to limit their impressions?" I asked.

"Exactly", said JFK. "The child's impressions of other creatures or things are often inaccurate or mistaken, and although maturity implies that one has mature impressions, that they can see others in their correct size and establish appropriate relationships, in most cases, these impressions are not mature at all, but are still as inaccurate and mistaken as those of a child."

"Then the adult's impressions are really childish ones?"

"No, they are not the same, since they are usually impressions which have been received on many previous occasions, whereas the child is often receiving them for the first time. The adult does establish correct or adequate conscious impressions of others insofar as those impressions are necessary to obtain the physical needs of food, shelter, clothing and procreation, as well as for the defense of the physical shell. A human has to establish a correct physical impressions of another human who is about to bash his head in with a club, or he may depart the physical life."

"You mentioned procreation. I suppose you include conscious impressions of sexual needs?"

"Yes. As a matter of fact, sexual needs are often accompanied by a heightened consciousness, a greater degree of awareness than is usual in the animal nature's seeking of food, clothing, and shelter. In respect to other impressions, however, they remain blurred and imprecise, even the impressions of those who are very close to each other for long periods of time. What this means is that most human adults have an imperfect, or childish impression of each other, and this, of course, affects their attempts at communication."

"And considering this widespread state of unconsciousness, and inadequate impressions, you still believe that I can go out and tell the world that the people who are alive are only partly conscious, that physical death is nothing to be feared, and that the relapse of the physical shell does not affect a person's real values?

"As I said before, you'll manage to do it."

"Admitting that I have an inquiring mind, how am I to remember all that we have talked about during these conversations?"

"That is the simplest part of it. When you are ready to set down our conversations, everything that we have said will appear before your eyes. It will seem to you that you are reading it off in clear print from a long, continuous printed page. You only have to copy it."

"I'm glad that is taken care of", I said. "After all, I could get a lot of this material confused, and perhaps do you more harm than good."

"No, I don't think that will happen, the way things are worked out", said JFK.

"It would be a lot to trust to one person's memory", I said. "I may be able to absorb a lot, but this has covered quite a bit of territory, and most of it refers to things that aren't usually discussed."

"That too is no accident", said JFK. "Just as man limits his range of conscious impressions, purely as a matter of physical comfort, he also excludes thoughts and ideas which would tend to stir him from his ordinary routines."

"There must be some immediate reason why you are doing this", I said. "After all, everything that we have gone over has been true for thousands of years. Why is it so important to go into it now?"

"There is a very important reason", said JFK. "Mankind has now reached a point of development where the delicate balance which makes life on earth possible is being affected, and even destroyed. There is grave danger that unless tremendous reforms take place very soon, not only mankind, but all forms of life on earth, both animate and inanimate, may disappear. This, in turn, will affect many other forms of being."

"Do you mean life on other planets?"

"Other planets, other dimensions, there are various modes of being, which we usually refer to simply as All Worlds. This situation has developed principally because of man's self-limited consciousness, so that he refuses to understand how far he has developed his capacity to alter and destroy his surroundings."

"But this dangers is not new, is it?" I asked. "It seemed to me that this probability has existed for some time."

"So it has", said JFK, "but the longer it exists, the more inevitable it becomes. The reason for the danger is quite simple. These tremendous capacities to alter, change and destroy his environment have been developed by only a small fraction of humanity, but these capacities are passing into the hands of many people who have no idea of the danger, or who are reckless enough not to care. For instance, the atomic bomb was invented by a small group of people, but the decisions as to whether to use it or not are left to people who had nothing to do with its development. After all, I had the power to order its use during certain emergencies; so did Eisenhower, and Truman did order its use, even though he had no prior knowledge of its destructive capabilities."

"Then you consider the atomic bomb the greatest threat to mankind?"

"Not necessarily. The atomic bomb is actually a rather clumsy form of energy, and one which would never have been developed had it not been for a peculiar chain of circumstances. The greater danger lies in the entire range of man's technological development, since these advances are in the hands of people who have limited impressions and who are only partly conscious. Most of the important inventions were produced by men who have already departed from the earth. Now that mankind has inherited these things, few people show any sense of responsibility as to their use. A few men developed the automobile, but millions of people recklessly risk their lives in them every day, in blind disregard of the way in which these machines should be handled. The same situation exists with respect to most of the other inventions. But an even greater danger is the tremendous increase in the numbers of mankind, a senseless proliferation which has also been made possible by technological advances. The fact is that even without the use of atomic weapons, the entire earth and its atmosphere is being poisoned by the rapid growth of humanity."

"I suppose another world war will be necessary to halt this proliferation?"

"Certainly not. As a matter of fact, wars seem to stimulate the increase in mankind, because the element of danger leads man to abandon his traditional mating practices, and to impregnate as many women as possible. In this case, however, a world war would soon become an atomic battle which would make most of the earth inhabitable. Even if atomic weapons were not used, according to prior agreements, that would not preclude the possibility, one might say, the certainty, that stores of atomic weapons might not be set off either by accident or by saboteurs."

"Then the earth is likely to be poisoned, or to become a desert, whether there is an atomic war or not?"

"That is the only possible future, under present conditions. That is why mankind must begin to understand itself, its manner of existence, and the reason for its existence. And that is why I have been allowed to lift the curtain of the mystery of death, but only a little."

"Then you are not really giving me the full answer to the oldest mystery of mankind", I asked, "the mystery of death?"

"That was never my intention", replied JFK. "You could say that I am not allowed to do so, or you could say that there are no terms with which I could explain it entirely to your satisfaction. In fact, much of what I have been telling you simply reaffirms many of man's oldest religious beliefs, and in particular, those of Christianity."

"Then you ought to restate those beliefs for me, as clearly as possible, so that I can reach the greatest number of people."

"The first one, and probably the oldest one", said JFK, "is simply this. There is no death. By that, we mean that there is no end to life, or that death is not the end of life. Life's card is simply turned over, and a new card is dealt. Of course, man has always known this instinctively. Life would be unbearable if one had to accept the realization that it would end so brutishly and so insensitively. However, the selfishness of the earthly shell and its insistence on its own importance has often obscured this realization. In the main, nothing that I will say in these conversations is alien to man's thought. He has been aware for many centuries that life transcends death. However, because of his limited consciousness and his inadequate impressions, man will find much of what I have to say very disturbing."

"There is no death. That reflects the thought of many religious leaders", I said.

"Yes, it does", said JFK. "The second idea is that the sort of life a man leads determines which his course after death will be. This too is a principle of most religious thought, although I intend in later conversations to go into it much deeper."

"So far, there is nothing very startling here", I said. "Life transcends death; individual morality affects one's after-life. I doubt if I'm going to shock anyone with these observations."

"But we are only making a beginning", said JFK. "Wait and see what sort of reception you get when you tell them that man must reconsider his entire position in the universe. It will be like the times of Galileo, when man had to accept the fact that the earth revolves around the sun, and that the earth is not the center of the universe. Now man must accept the fact that not only is he a limited form of consciousness and intelligence, but he is far from being the most highly developed form of life. Man must also accept the fact that life on earth is not a particularly desirable stage of existence, although I believe that most of the world's population will be inclined to agree. The brutal truth is that life on earth is a sort of Purgatory, a stage of suspension or punishment, in the universal sweep of life. This too has long been known to man, but he has suppressed it. It is a truth, but it is not an absolute truth, in the sense that life is a Truth, or that the universe is a Truth."

"Do you mean that it is not an all-embracing truth?" I asked.

"It is not a permanent truth, or an established truth", answered JFK, "that is to say, it has not been added to the store of unalterable truths which make up the universe. We are now beginning to touch upon the true importance of earth. In stating that it is a Purgatory, I have to warn you that this also is a flexible concept. A life on earth can be a higher stage of being, or it can be a lower one. For some of those from other modes of being, a life on earth is like a sentence to Devil's Island, because they have retrogressed or because they have offended the purest sensibilities of the mode of being to which they had formerly arisen. For others, a life on earth is a tremendous step upward, comparable to the emergence of the dump amphibian who established himself upon land and became a literate, articulate creature. And for still others, a life on earth is their only opportunity of redemption; it is not a punishment, or a chance to improve, but rather a chance to save themselves from a blind and silent Eternity. Consequently, lives on earth are lived for varying reasons and with varying intensity. The value of earth in the scheme of things is that it can be so many things for so many differing modes of being. No other part of All Worlds is able to offer this, because values elsewhere are fixed, rather than flexible. And it is this key role which is now threatened by the proliferation of mankind."

"But couldn't this be controlled by limiting the number of individuals who are sent to earth?"

"Many of them are not sent", replied JFK. "Some of them arrive there by accident, others are escaping punishment elsewhere, but the most important thing to remember is that many banished higher modes of being, as well as lower ones, appear on earth as groups of life, rather than as individuals. These groups are allowed to exercise great autonomy in living with each other, and consequently they indulge themselves by attacking each other and attempting to destroy each other in what Darwin supposed was the struggle for survival of the fittest, but which is really the presence of so much of the evil of the universe here on earth. As Darwin discovered, some forms of life which appeared on earth were subsequently overcome and destroyed, and they have vanished. What he did not know was that many other forms also have appeared and disappeared, and most of them are gone without a trace. This is also true of some mighty civilizations of the past, which have not left so much as a pile of rubble, although some memory of them survives in ancient legends."

"Then the danger can't be as great as you say", I observed. "If other forms have vanished, why can't man destroy himself and disappear without anyone being unduly concerned?"

"No previous form of life which appeared on earth developed the power to destroy, not only its enemies, but itself and the earth as well", said JFK. "Should the earth be destroyed, this means that the universe would lose its safety valve, and that forces which had proven too dangerous in other modes of being could no longer be banished. The universe would no longer have the prison, the experimental station, the cocoon, which the earth has been in the past. Also, the rest of the universe would miss the earth for a rather unflattering reason."

"Oh, well, let's hear it", I said.

"First of all", said JFK, "you must realize that life on earth assumes greater varieties and forms than anywhere else in the universe. This is because the forms of life on earth stem from so many sources, the rejects of other worlds, criminals, imperfect forms, etc. For this very reason, the rest of the universe finds the spectacle of life on earth a continuous source of entertainment."

"Do you mean that the earth really is a sort of zoo for the universe?"

"You could call it that. You could also call it an insane asylum, a prison, a crucible; oh, it is any one of a number of things. That's why the rest of the universe has become so accustomed to observing life on earth, and why it would be so greatly missed."

"It's just a big television show, eh?"

"You could say that."

"You make life on earth sound much more interesting", I said. "With all this going on, I wonder why we are spending so much time in front of our television sets. The programs get duller all the time."

"It seems to be a form of hypnotism", said JFK. "Of course man has always prized unreality above all else."

"Why is that?" I asked.

"He wants to escape from himself", said JFK. "Considering his origins, is that so surprising?"

"No", I replied, "and the conditions of life for most humans are such that one can hardly blame them for seeking unreality in any guise."

"Nevertheless, this desire to escape himself has only created more and greater problems for man", said JFK.

"Do you mean that he imagines problems for himself which are worse than the ones he has to face in real life?" I asked.

"No", said JFK. "In attempting to escape his own nature, man merely aggravates the problems which he tries to avoid. Most of man's problems today are those which have been created by his attempt to escape. That is why the first precept of any intelligent system of philosophy is 'Know thyself'. Man's refusal to face himself opens all sorts of abysses into which he inevitably falls."

"Is that the legendary 'fall of man', then", I asked, "the pitfalls of his flight from himself."

"No, the 'fall of man' refers to the banishment to earth of one of the higher modes of being which produced man", said JFK. "The 'fall of man' does not refer directly to man, but to the form, the god, one might say, from which man issued as the result of the fall."

"But if man's nature is so terrible", I said, "how can man dare to face himself?"

"This is the confrontation which must take place", said JFK, "If man, and the earth, are to survive. Let us look at one aspect of this. The newspapers print accounts of horrible murders, many of them committed by people who had no previous criminal records. These murderers, like everyone else on earth, are people who have refused to face their own natures, and who, nevertheless, were fully aware of what they were."

"Are all men potential murderers, then?"

"Not necessarily", said JFK. "The origins of some groups are more violent and terrible than those of others, but as a general statement, one must go on the premise that any man is capable of any atrocity. At the same time, men try to compensate for this knowledge of their selves by speaking of the divine in their natures, and by pretending to be what they are not."

"Is there nothing of the divine in man?"

"The divine is in every man", said JFK. "However, if man were absolutely divine, he would not be existing on earth, and if there were nothing of the divine in him, he would not be existing on earth."

"I think I can understand why man prefers unreality to reality", I said, "even an unreality as monotonous as that of television programs. I was talking to a recent immigrant from Europe, who was quite concerned about the rising crime rate in our cities. He had seen a few television programs, and he suggested to me, quite seriously, that offenders be sentenced to watch at least six hours of television programs every day. When I told him that a large percentage of people were already watching television six hours a day, he refused to believe me."

"I don't think I could spare much time for it", said JFK.

"By the way", I said, "do you think you will be making another sojourn on earth?"

"I certainly hope not", said JFK. "At the present time, that largely depends on you."

"I'm still dubious about whether I have a necessary role in this", I said. "It seems to me that since you now occupy some sort of a supernatural position, you could handle this much more easily yourself. Couldn't you just wave your hand and have a million books printed which would se forth everything you had to say?"

"That's another popular misconception", said JFK. "As a matter of fact, people from other modes of being have practically no influence in the earthly sphere. Because of the very nature of the sources of life on earth, its physics were made extremely rigorous, so that those from other modes of being could not assist or interfere with those who were exiled there. As a result, we are excluded from visiting or interfering in the affairs of earth. This can only be done by accepting a new earthly shell and by undergoing another complete sojourn on earth. As you can understand, those in other modes of being do not wish to do this."

"That brings up another question", I said. "Many people on earth believe that we have been getting visitors from other planets."

"There have been a few", said JFK, "but only a very few. There were some incurable curiosity-seekers whose recklessness drove them to risk the dangers of seeing the place for themselves. They were always too terrified to make any contact with people on earth, and at the first sight of a human, they usually took off at top speed. You must remember, too, that earth is off limits for the rest of the universe, and that the dangers of visiting there are very great. Nevertheless, there have been expeditions which went to earth for the purpose of capturing slaves or specimens. They snared quite a number on one occasion, I believe they took the entire crew of a ship, but on most occasions they seized a single specimen in some remote area and left immediately."

"Why should they be so terrified of humans?" I asked. "After all, they did represent higher modes of being."

"Of course they had superior arms", said JFK, "and there was really nothing to fear, but they often panicked at the sight of humans. That's principally due to the many legends about earth which have been repeated for thousands of years. And since it is a forbidden place, there are a great many exaggerations and preposterous myths, which are firmly believed in many parts of the universe."

"I don't think my chances are very good of carrying out this assignment", I said. "Do you really think that I can win over the support of any sizeable group of people by telling them that they live in Purgatory?"

"Perhaps it hasn't been put that bluntly to them", said JFK, "but you will find that most of them are already aware of it. Even for the most fortunate of humans, life is hardly a feast of caviar!"

"I doubt if they will take kindly to the doctrine that they are exiles and criminals from other modes of life", I said.

"If they don't, it won't be because they haven't been prepared for it", said JFK. "I'm speaking now about one of the most fundamental doctrines of Christianity, original sin."

"But original sin refers to the sin of the first man, Adam", I said.

"That is the way the theologians have always presented it", said JFK, "nor can one blame them. It is much simpler than to go into the origins of life on earth, even if the theologians were aware of those origins. Some of them were aware of it, because there were documents which described the actual conditions of the fall, but now the story has receded from the consciousness of man. Today's theologians seem to have no memory of the original sin, which was man's heritage of crime and evil from the rest of the universe."

"I must say that you have an answer for everything", I said. "I ought not to admit it, but you have me convinced, if only for the moment."

"I've been told that I was a rather good persuader, in my day", said JFK. "We seem to have taken this about as far as we can for the time being. Let's call it a day, and I'll get in touch with you again."

"All right", I said, "But I hope you haven't lost sight of the fact that I'm still human. I have a limited life span and I may not be around more than a few score years."

"Don't worry about that", said JFK. "I still know what time is."

The radiance around him slowly faded. I began to struggle against a rough hand which had seized me by the shoulder.

"Don't seem to be anything wrong with you", said a red-faced farmer. He was leaning in the car window while he shook me awake. "I went by here a couple of hours ago, and you haven't moved a muscle since then. I thought maybe you'd passed out."

"Nothing like that", I said. "I've been working pretty hard, and I just thought I'd take a snooze."

"Shouldn't be surprised if you don't have a stiff neck tomorrow", he said, "the way your head was laying across the window. I don't see how anybody could rest in that position."

"When I'm tired", I said, "I just drop. I certainly feel rested."

"I know you've been here since 2:30", he said, "and now it's almost five. Look, if you're sure you're okay, I've got to get my cows in."

"I'm fine", I said. "Thanks for looking in on me."

Now I had told my first lie about this occurrence, and I began to wonder when, if ever, I should start telling the truth. That is, if I knew what the truth was. My recollection was very clear. I had had a conversation with the late John F. Kennedy. When I began to recall what we had been talking about, my mind seemed to go blank. I was still aware of the lingering effects of the radiance, and a wonderful sense of well-being, but it disturbed me that I could remember nothing of the conversation. He had said that he would help me to remember. I closed my eyes, concentrated, and at once a printed page appeared in front of me, each word easily legible. I began to read it.

"You look rather foolish."

The rest of the conversation followed, line after line. I read for a few minutes, and decided this was no place to stay. I opened my eyes, started the Buick, and drove away. Other people besides the farmer must have seen me parked there all afternoon. I didn't relish having a state trooper drive up to ask me what I was waiting for.

Conversation Two

On the night after this conversation, I lay awake for hours, thinking over this new and puzzling experience. There was no problem to transcribing the conversations, and the easiest solution seemed to be that I do what John F. Kennedy asked. I had only to get up, go downstairs, and begin the job. Nevertheless, I found myself resisting this, for several reasons. First of all, I saw little likelihood that any sizeable portion of humanity would welcome the news that it was of criminally insane origins. The resentment at this statement would, of course, be directed at me rather than at John F. Kennedy, even if anyone were willing to believe that this doctrine ha come from him.

Second, the news that humanity was on the verge of destroying itself and the earth would not come as a surprise to anyone who was sufficiently literate to read the daily press. Indeed, mankind had lived with this knowledge for so long that his major problem was how to settle down and live with the situation, while he waited for it all to end as quietly and as painlessly as possible, "not with a bang but a whimper".

The revelation that the earth served as a sort of comedy relief for the rest of the universe seemed unlikely to win any friends for me, nor would it restore meaningful purpose to the lives of mankind. Viewing the situation objectively, it seemed to me that fate had merely offered me another blind alley, discouragingly similar to the ones I had been walking in all my life. From a purely selfish standpoint, I could see no reason why I should make any effort whatsoever to carry out JFK's mandate. After all, he had merely affirmed the basic tenets by which millions of thinking, religious humans lived; original sin, morality during life, and a life after death. Even though he had offered some new perspective on these things, and even though he had made a somewhat miraculous appearance after death, there was still only a remote chance that I or any other human could construct a new and more viable program for improving the lot of mankind from these tenets. That such a program could now avert universal disaster seemed out of the question.

Putting the JFK dilemma out of my mind, I continued to lead my rather meaningless life, enjoying fewer rewards than most, but my lot was not as grim or hopeless as the lot of those who occupied the greater portion of the earth. I ate the meat and cursed the bread", and, although I was aware that there were millions of humans for whom meat represented impossible wealth, it did not make mine taste any better. Mankind continued to proliferate, the water became more polluted, foodstuffs more adulterated, slums more hideous, and the threat of atomic disaster more appalling.

Several weeks after my initial conversation with JFK, I had my second encounter with him. It was a quiet Sunday morning, and I was alone in the house. My mother and my sister had gone to church, and I was dawdling about, comfortably contemplating the carrying out of several small tasks which I really had no intention of doing. I stretched out on a couch, and one again I entered into the radiance. JFK seemed rather annoyed.

"You aren't very anxious to help me out, are you?" he said.

"I'm not very anxious to do anything", I replied, "but if you can give me some worthwhile reason for going ahead on this, I'll be glad to help.

I would appreciate it, though, if you'd let me ask a few more questions about my part in this."

"Go ahead", said JFK.

"I'm still uncertain about your reasons for choosing me."

"That's simple enough", said JFK. "I knew you wouldn't start climbing the walls the moment I appeared. You're not surprised at anything, are you?"

"That wasn't always true", I said, "but the past few years, I've seen so much that it would take quite a lot to startle me."

"And you have reached a sort of dead end, that is, things look rather hopeless, don't they?"

"They are no more hopeless for me than they are for millions of others", I said.

"That's not quite true", said JFK, "because you had always hoped to do a great deal more than those millions of others."

"Perhaps you're right", I said.

"And there isn't much chance that you will, as things look at the present time?"

"Not much."

"So little, in fact, that you have contemplated ending it all."

"I've thought about it, yes. There didn't seem to be any reason why I shouldn't, but at the same time, I couldn't see any reason why I should."

"But there was every reason why you should", said JFK, "that is, if you were determined to maintain your previous standards, and if you had stuck to your previous goals. What you really decided was that you would no longer demand so much more from life than other people, and that you would scale your demands down to their level."

"That's about the size of it", I said. "It's an adjustment that most people have to make, at some point in their lives."

"And isn't that a kind of suicide? You didn't kill yourself, but you did begin to kill off your goals."

"You're getting ahead of me, but when I catch up, I probably will have to admit that you're right."

"I didn't go into this before", said JFK, "but a large part of what I want to go over with you is concerned with just this dilemma, death-in-life, the effect of people on each other, mass murder, inner slavery, a lot of things."

"It does sound interesting."

"And also, there is something in it for you", said JFK. "You will have the opportunity to restore some of your original goals, that is, you will have the chance to do something meaningful, if you will go along with me on this."

"So, even from another world, you can still offer only earthly rewards", I said. "Isn't that rather Satanic?"

"That depends largely on you", said JFK.

"Touché", I said. "And from your vantage point, in scamming the several billion inhabitants of the earth, you decided that a disheartened average American would be the ideal instrument for your purposes?"

"Not quite", said JFK. "I picked you out because you are an artist."

"It's very kind of you to say so", I replied. "And I might as well point out that you are the first. Even though I have been painting for ten years, I still haven't gotten the least acknowledgement."

"That means one of two things", said JFK. "Either you are very good, or you are very bad. In either case, your work must be outstanding."

"Thanks for leaving me right where I was", I said.

"It was an important thing to me, this matter of our being an artist", said JFK, "because I'm going to tell you something I've never told any human being before."

"What is that?" I asked. "I supposed that everything possible was already known about you, considering all of the publicity you received."

"Not this", said JFK. "The fact is that the only thing I ever wanted desperately in my life, was to be an artist."

"I can't understand why you didn't do it", I said. "You had every opportunity. You could have had it all, the studio on the Left bank, discreet gifts to the critics, perhaps a silent partnership in a good gallery, everything that is needed to get the work off the ground. It would have cost your father much less than a political career."

"No, no, no", said JFK. "I'm talking about many years ago, when I was a child. I had this terrific desire to paint, and at the same time, I hesitated to mention it to anyone, because it was so far removed from anything in our lives. I knew it would be something that my father wouldn't approve. That is one of my earliest and my strongest recollections. I was tempting myself, thinking about brushing those colors onto a canvas, making a vision of the world, and do you know what happened? My brothers called me out to play football. I was still dreaming about how wonderful it would be to paint when the ball was snapped back against my chest and knocked the wind out of me. Then I was getting bawled out for not keeping my eyes open during the play. Father didn't say anything, but I noticed that he was staring at me, almost as if he was reading my mind. I knew then that if I ever dared to say anything to him about becoming an artist, he would always be looking at me with the same reproachful look, that I would be letting him and the family down. So I jumped up, grabbed the ball, and made a wild run with it. That was the last time that I ever let myself dream about the artist's life."

"You never mentioned it to him?"

"Not to him, nor to anyone else. I was still conscious of that tremendous desire, buried deep within myself, and as far as possible, I avoided art for years. I pretended to have little interest in paintings, and I ignored art classes. I put the whole thing out of my mind."

"And you accuse me of committing suicide, killing off my goals."

"Perhaps that's why I brought it up. Of course, I might have been able to go into it, at one point."

"When was that?"

"After I had become President. I was my own man then, but it was too late. It wouldn't have been a case of my father looking over my shoulder, it would have been the entire country!"

"Painting while Rome burns, eh?"

"Something of the sort. Even if I had taken it up them, I was afraid of becoming a painter of the Eisenhower type, picking out little still lifes like an old lady doing needlework. Perhaps you can understand now that I was cut off in more ways than one."

"You really believe that your father would never have approved an art career?"

"I certainly lived with him long enough", said JFK. "It would have been too slow. I don't want to sound callous, but he was the kind of man who had to see a real return on his investments. He would never have been able to sit on his hands for twenty years while I developed as a painter."

"Then he considered you as investments?"

"Not in a cold-blooded sense. It was simply a manner of looking at things that he had developed, and that affected everything around him. He could glance at us and compute in a minute just what he had invested in us. He could also compute a fair estimate of how we would perform in a given situation."

"Do you mean that he expected a return from you just as he did his other investments?"

"I think every parent expects some return", said JFK, "but with him it was a little more than that. And he didn't like long term investments. He wanted an early return. That's why we had to make good in a hurry."

"But long term investments sometimes bring in a bigger yield", I said.

"I know that", said JFK. "I remember that he was always being offered paintings during the 1920s. I found out later that they were Van Goghs, Monets, he could have picked them up for about a thousand dollars apiece. Today, they're worth a hundred times that much. Of course, he did make that great a return on some of his investments, but he wouldn't buy painting because he didn't know enough about them, and he didn't want to trust anybody else's judgement. He had no eye for paintings. I don't suppose any of us did."

"There could have been plenty of prestige in your becoming an artist", I said.

"No, our money was too new", said JFK. "If we were the Phippses, I could have gone into orchid-raising, no one would have cared, but we had to make our mark. Besides, for an Irish Catholic from Boston, there are only two roads open, the Church of politics."

"Or both", I said. "Your father never considered any of you for business?"

"Financial dynasties don't work too well, and they don't last very long", said JFK. "Father once told me that if the Harriman boys hadn't gotten out of business and gone into politics, the Union Pacific money wouldn't have lasted them twenty years."

"Was he afraid you and your brothers might have the same problems?"

"Not really. It wasn't necessary for us to make any more money. Father is really a very shrewd person. He wanted very much for each of us to make our own success. In business, we would have had to be measured against him, and it would have been very difficult to top his success, or even to equal it, after the record he had made. We might have done well enough, but he wanted more than that. I doubt if we would have made the killings he dis."

"Why not?"

"Because a killing is just that. You have to kill off a lot of people's hopes and ambitions to make a million dollars. It doesn't happen in a vacuum, you know. Father knew that we hadn't developed the killer instinct."

"I should think Bobby would have it", I said.

"Bobby's killer instinct is a myth", said JFK. "He's too reckless, and winning means too much to him. You see, you don't really gamble in the world of finance. You set up a duck and you blast hell out of it. It's not a very sporting game, and most of the people in it are ducks who would like to become hunters. Very few of them make it."

"You don't seem to like businessmen any more that your father did."

"Father once told me that they had great charm and beautiful manners, speaking of the old Boston crowd, until they had maneuvered you into a position where your jugular vein was exposed. Joe could have handled himself among them, but the rest of us, it would have been touch and go. Father made sure that we'd never have the chance to find out. It was rather intelligent of him to push us into public careers, where we would be on our own, and not measured so much against his achievements."

"But he had quite a public career", I said. "What about the Security Exchange Commission, Ambassador to Great Britain, those were important posts."

"They were appointive offices. He wasn't elected to them. I doubt if he could have been."

"Why not?"

"Because he had trained himself to measure everything in dollars. As a result, dollars became his only means of communication. That's fine for getting things done, but people won't vote for a dollar."

"I always thought they would. Bread and circuses."

"Bread and circuses, yes, dollars, no. My father had become a dollar sign to the American people, and no matter what's at stake, the people won't vote for that. You can't nape a single Presidential candidate in the past fifty years who was a dollar sign. Hoover came closest, but he concealed his money-grubbing behind the story of the Belgian

Food campaign. The dollar-hunter concealed himself behind the façade of the great humanitarian."

"You father seriously wanted the Presidency at one time, didn't he?"

"He wanted it for a long time, but he is a realist, and he finally understood that the American people will never vote for a money man. That's why he was so careful to keep us out of the market-place. Besides, it would have been anti-climactic. His real career had already fulfilled itself in business. It would have been disastrous for us to go into finance and try to compete against the record he had made. As it worked out, we were able to do the things he hadn't been able to do, win public support, and be elected to office."

"He was certainly no Roosevelt when it came to arousing popular support, was he? I suppose that was a matter of his personality?"

"Well, I never saw any crowds dancing in the streets when he rode by, or strewing roses, roses in his path. He really had nothing to offer the electorate, except his unsurpassed knowledge of how to make profits, and governments don't make profits."

"You and your brothers certainly rang a change on his themes. You gave the American people youth, vitality and hope."

"We did create that image. Of course, it was what we set out to do. That was the principal reason why Father stayed in the background. It wasn't that we were trying to repudiate him."

"How do you think Johnson is doing?"

"He's doing all right. Of course, he's only carrying out the role he has always played, the parliamentarian. He's not really an executive, and so he is a rather transitory figure. The most he can do is to try to hold the pieces together for a little longer. At any rate, it doesn't matter very much, because he will soon be with me."

"That doesn't sound too good for him."

"On the contrary, it's his way out, just as it may have been mine."

"How did you really decide on him for Vice-President?"

"He was forced on me."

"I have a slight confession to make", I said. "I didn't vote for you."

"There's not much point in my getting upset about that, is there?"

"I didn't vote against you, either", I said. "I didn't vote at all, not from any conviction one way or the other, but because I dislike doing useless things. But from your new point of view, what sort of future do you see for America?"

"America no longer has a future, unless the world has a future, and that brings us back to what I want you to do."

"Congratulations. I see now that all of these personal interjections had a solid purpose, intended to prepare me for the struggle."

"You have had some doubts as to whether I really am John F. Kennedy", he said. "I thought that a few comments like these might help you to resolve them."

"Consider them resolved", I said. "I'm convinced that this isn't some sort of hallucination. You still have the advantage of me in one respect. You seem to be sure that there is a chance of accomplishing your purpose. I only wish I were sure of it."

"There is a very good chance. Mankind isn't suicidal by nature, even though many of his actions seem to indicate it. The very fact that mankind continues to survive in the face of seemingly insurmountable problems proves that there is still hope. It is that hope which is our greatest asset."

"Isn't that what all of the prophets have tried to offer, hope?"

"Not all of them", said JFK. "Some of them were merely Cassandras, pointing out oncoming disasters which anyone could have foreseen. The ones whose names have survived, however, were the ones who offered genuine hope to mankind."

"You mentioned in our last conversation that Christ was the most important of the prophets because He was the one who remained most true to Himself. I wish you could go into that further."

"I intend to. I had also mentioned that some of the other great prophets, Zoroaster, Buddha,

Confucius and Mohammed, did not accomplish as much, for a very simple reason. Each of these prophets was to some extent flawed, even though each of them pursued with great clarity and great success his personal vision of the truth. For instance, Buddha exhausted the physical possibilities of the body before becoming a mystic. He enjoyed women, fine food, wine, the pleasures of a physical existence which were available to a worldly prince. Confucius spent much of his life in civic affairs, that is, he was a public official. Mohammed became a military man. Only Christ remained aloof from all of these earthly pursuits throughout His life. Physical abandonment, government and war, these are all integral part of the mass man's life. No prophet can touch them without the risk of compromising his mission."

"Then you demand asceticism of a truly great prophet."

"It is not what I demand. It is what the task demands. One cannot perfect one's vision as an individual by indulging in these things, because the universal view of mankind may be affected by the smallest occurrence in one's life. It may be difficult for you to understand that only the most absolute individual can attain a truly universal view."

"I think I can understand that."

"Then you may also understand that the idea of the individual is the contribution of the earth to the universe. Such a concept was unknown until it was developed there, through a fortuitous chain of accidents."

"And Christ was the one who perfected the individual view?"

"Yes."

"What about theory of His divinity?"

"He said that He was the Son of God. Doesn't that establish his divinity?"

"It does if you accept Him."

"And why shouldn't you accept Him?"

"I think I have. But what about the problems of divinity for the rest of mankind?"

"Christ said that He was the Son of God. He did not say that all men were not the Sons of God."

"Then you not only affirm His divinity, but you also extend that divinity to embrace the rest of mankind."

"Not at all. True divinity for mankind is only a possibility. It was a reality for Christ because He affirmed it for Himself, He remained true to Himself and to the divinity which was His true self."

"Then you are saying that the divinity in oneself is really one's individuality?"

"It is much more complex than that, but that will do for a beginning. One's individual being is also but a possibility, in most cases. You might realize that Christ was not so intent upon mankind accepting His divinity as He was anxious for them to discover the divinity in themselves, the spark of the divine which was their birthright to an existence as an individual."

"Then all we have to do to become divine is to assert ourselves as individuals."

"It isn't quite that easy, but that is a necessary step. Asserting oneself as an individual does not mean that one automatically becomes an individual, or that one becomes an individual right away. It does mean that one opens the door to one's individual divinity. You may remember that Christ travelled a long and lonely road, as anyone must do who wishes to win for himself that prize of earthly existence, one's attainment of true individuality."

"Then we must affirm the existence of God by affirming our individual existence?"

"That also is one step, but not the only one."

"One thing has puzzled me for years. There is a growing belief that Christ's ascension after the Crucifixion was more physical than we realized on earth, and that he actually entered a space ship and travelled to another plane."

"That was not necessary", said JFK.

"What is God in the plane of existence in which you are now?" I asked. "Have you become joined to Him, are you co-existent with Him, or how would you describe it?"

"I cannot describe it, because the relationship which man can achieve with God is quite different from the existence which I now occupy."

"You speak of attainment of true individuality as the most important aim of earthly existence. Does this mean that the individual represents the greatest good on earth?"

"He represents the great possibility of good", said JFK.

"If the individual represents a positive force for good", I said, "doesn't that mean that group are evil?"

"Groups of men are not necessarily evil", said JFK, "but they multiply man's capacity for evil by a fantastic ratio. The individual capacity for good is almost unlimited, as the life of Christ demonstrates, which the group capacity for evil is also unlimited, as the invention of the atomic bomb demonstrates. It would have been completely beyond the ability of any individual to invent or to build an atomic bomb. As a matter of fact, it took the cooperation of thousands of people, over quite a long period of time."

"But you were a typical member of many groups during your life on earth. Now you criticize groups as evil", I said.

"I have not transcended life merely to be committed or defined forever by my activities on earth", said JFK. "If that were true, there would be no point in our having these conversations. Of course I was an active member of many groups, I was prominent as a Catholic layman, an active member of the United States Army, a leader of the Democratic Party, to name only a few."

"And from your present viewpoint you define these groups as essentially evil by their nature or their activities?"

"Of course not. I am saying that man must reaffirm his individuality if he is to survive. He cannot affirm his individuality as a member of a group. Anyone who is thought of primarily as a member of a group, and only secondarily, if at all, as an individual, has already lost much of his chance to do good on earth, and has thereby become a contributing factor to the general degrading of life on earth."

"Then the groups degrade the individual?" I asked.

"All life degrades", said JFK. "This is an essential process of life. One of the functions of individuality is to react to that degrading in a discontinuous manner, whereas group life accepts the degrading as a matter of course, without attempting to react to it."

"Is the constant degrading of life the primary cause of people losing their individuality and sinking into the hopelessness of group existence?"

"One might say that fear and insecurity are as important a cause", replied JFK, "and that humans feel that group life affords them greater possibilities of a satisfactory existence. However, fear and insecurity have always been part of man's life on earth. In the past, he had greater courage, and he faced these fears as an individual. It was said that man could be defeated but not destroyed. Now, apparently, this is changing. Man is no longer being defeated, but he is in danger of being destroyed. Much of this is attributable of the growth of group existence. Man has been persuaded, although in his heart he knows this is wrong, that he will be more secure if he faces his problems as a member of a group. In reality, the moment he does this, he opens the door to his own destruction."

"But it's quite natural to suppose that a hundred men, acting together in their own interest, would be safer than one man struggling alone", I said.

"Only if one forgets that the true value of life on earth is the one man struggling alone", said JFK. "Mass communication are causing men to forget these things; these forces denigrate the individual and exalt the group. You see, the formation of groups is a reversion to the basis of life on earth, the evil forces which were exiled here from other modes of being and which made their appearance on earth as groups of life. An amazing thing happened, something which astounded the universe. Individuals began to evolve from these evil groups who were capable of tremendous good; obviously, some remote capacity for good existed even in the most evil forces, and the earth proved to be the catalyst which allowed this good to overcome its evil origins. Now, the opposite is happening. Just when the universe was marveling at this unpredictable occurrence, and congratulating itself that a new and healthier opportunity for life had become available, the process began to reverse itself; the strong, courageous and good individuals began to revert to the original group evils which had spawned them; it seems that they are reclaiming their own."

"And you hope to restore the individual by explaining to him what he is and where he comes from?"

"Since he seems incapable of knowing this himself, it is imperative that he be told."

"But you had said earlier that man instinctively knows already, what he is and where he comes from", I said.

"Everything is known", said JFK. "There are no secrets in the universe. But what is known can be obscured or disguised. It is like the mysterious cocoon, which opens to become a beautiful butterfly. As everything in the universe is reversible, the life of man has become the reverse of the cocoon. Born all-knowing, throughout his life he spins a cocoon around himself, so that by the time he has come to die he has become an ultimate mystery."

"Is that what is called the innocence of childhood", I asked, "this state of all-knowing?"

"Of course", said JFK. "Instead of becoming a revelation, man's life devolves into a more and more complex mystification, while at the same time he is uneasily aware of what he is losing. It is for this reason that the evolvement of life known as "genius", that is, the fully aware man, is always tormented by the knowledge that he is on the verge of discovering the secret of the universe, that a curtain will be lifted and he will be dazzled by the transcendent beauty of All-Being."

"I had supposed that that revelation was the moment of death", I said, "the lifting of the curtain, and the attainment of all knowledge."

"No, the revelation which comes with death is another thing entirely", said JFK. "But why should one who has denied himself the revelation of life expect to receive the revelation of death? To live one's lifetime and ignore the moment of truth, to stand beside the curtain for many years and never once allow oneself to look beyond it, is this the manner in which an individual, one who is true to himself, proves himself?"

"There seem to be many forces in life which prevent the individual from looking beyond the curtain", I said. "Surely the individual cannot be blamed entirely."

"Certainly there are many forces which do not wish the individual to look beyond the curtain", said JFK, "and that is why I have been talking so much about groups. It is the group which does not wish the individual from looking beyond the curtain, because the group is satisfied with itself and the way things are. The group complacently accepts itself as the ultimate good, ignoring the fact that the group is a violation of mathematical law."

"How is that?" I asked.

"The group is less than the sum of its parts", said JFK. "That is to say, the group is a lesser value than any one of the individual values which compose it."

"But aren't these groups composed of individuals? Weren't you an individual when you were President of the United States?" I asked.

"The President of the United States has no opportunity to be an individual", said JFK. "After all, he can only reach that eminence by placing himself wholly at the disposal of groups. Do you know what Truman said when Eisenhower became President? Truman said, 'Eisenhower will issue an order to correct a given situation, and several days will go by, and nothing will have been done, and Eisenhower won't know why." I had no opportunity to assert myself as an individual when I was President. Most of my time was spent in trying to get people to cooperate with one another."

"I thought that was the purpose of groups, to promote cooperation."

"On the surface, that is the raison d'être of every group, but when you examine the record, you see that the principal function of every group is to promote itself at the expense of the individual. Why do you suppose that the multimillion dollars foundations in the United States, which have spent billions of dollars, have never once produced a good artist? It is because the true artist is an individual. Why haven't the universities, who also spend billions of dollars, produced any scholars? Because the scholar is an individual who embarks upon a voyage of discovery, and it is up to the university, a group, to sink his ship and toss him a life preserver, with a line attached to it, of course, when he comes up gasping for breath."

"Then you would describe the directors of these foundations and universities as essentially evil?"

"These directors are themselves individuals, of course", said JFK, "but they are individuals who have been fatally wounded or crippled by life, men who at one time had great hopes of achieving a career as individuals, and who were shot down as soon as they took to the air. Now that they have given up all hope of becoming artists or writers or of doing anything significant, they join wholeheartedly in the campaign of the groups to destroy all individuals. You might remember that no one is so sincere an apostle for slavery as a slave."

"Then these men are the sworn enemies of the individual?"

"That has become their only purpose in life", said JFK, "to reduce all men to the same sorry estate to which they have fallen. By doing this, they are contributing enormously to the problems of our time, which can only be solved by individuals. It is true that all of the groups are adding to these problems, and in many cases, they have created them, so that you could say they are evil in that respect."

"You seem to be saying that groups create the problems of mankind, and that individuals solve them?"

"That's one definition of the turn which life has taken in modern times."

"Then you are really attacking the philosophy of pluralism", I said. "This is the ruling doctrine of modern man, in which everything is left to the decisions of groups and committees, and nothing can be done without the active approval of corporations, foundations, universities, government departments, religious fractions, and even alliances of gangsters."

"Yes", said JFK, "it is strange indeed that not one man in a thousand has ever heard the world 'pluralism', and yet everyone in the modern world, with the possible exception of a few natives in Tierra del Fuego, is ruled by a pluralist coalition. In this respect, Russia and the United States are very similar, but they are not strikingly dissimilar from any other country in the world. In every case, the government represents a truce between powerful groups, the army, the church, the labor unions, or what have you. But no matter what their differences, they are all agreed upon one thing — to enslave the individual, and if he resists, to destroy him."

"And you attribute the plight of modern man to the activities of these groups?"

"Yes. You see, each of these groups owes its existence to a major problem in the life of the people. The army exists because of the fear of foreign domination; the labor unions exist because of labor problems; the religious groups exist because of man's fears about his manner of life and death. The directors of these groups always operate from one basic premise — that no problem must ever be solved, because, with the solution of the problem, the group would no longer have a right to exist. Knowing this, the directors of each group do their best to aggravate the problems of the individual, and to frustrate the efforts of individuals to solve them. Only in this way can the groups assure themselves of continued power and existence."

"It sounds as though you are advocating a return to individual government, one-man rule, a dictatorship or possible monarchy."

"Of course not. The career of Adolf Hitler proved that one-man rule proposes greater dangers to the people than pluralist rule, as far as the safety and well-being of the people is concerned."

"Were you aware of any of this when you were President?"

"I realized that as President, if I were to function at all, I must function with the support and consent of the pluralist powers", said JFK, "but I did not think beyond that. I knew that I could not afford to offend any one of these groups, and of course, if you are unable to do anything which will offend any one of a number of forces, your hands or more or less tied."

"And what kind of government are you advocating?" I asked.

"I'm not really advocating any kind of government, with its vicious practice of aggravating all of the problems of mankind, has to go. A group of intelligent, responsible individuals would be much more preferable."

"An oligarchy?"

"A small group of individuals who rule do not necessarily become an oligarchy. An oligarchy is a small group of men who act solely in order to further their own selfish interests. As I said, I'm not really advocating any particular form of government is best which governs least. I am merely criticizing pluralist government and advocating individual responsibility. This means an enormous task of re-education for all mankind, and it is one which all of the pluralist groups, and especially the universities, will unite solidly against."

"You make my proposal sound much more difficult", I said. "How can you awaken the individual if all of these powerful groups ally to prevent it?"

"They will recognize the danger", said JFK. "You may be sure of that before you begin."

"It sounds somewhat illogical", I said. "These groups have developed as the enemies of mankind, determined to destroy the individual, when they are composed entirely of individuals."

"That is true", said JFK. "Each member of a group is really his own worst enemy insofar as he supports the group. As John Donne said, 'Each man is an island'. What is done to one is done to all. An infringement upon one individual's liberties is an infringement upon everyone's liberties, but the groups commit such infringements with impunity. The basic tenet of every group, no matter what its professed creed may be, is that the individual has no rights. Not only does the group hate the individual, it also wishes to destroy the individual's self-respect, and the respect which others have for him. Consequently, the groups function with startling similarities. If you go to work for the Communist Party, the first thing you have to learn is that the Party is everything and the individual is nothing. If you go to work for Standard Oil, the first thing you learn is that the company is everything, and the individual is nothing. If you go to work for the Ford Foundation, the first thing you learn is that the foundation is everything, and the individual is nothing."

"Then it is possible to be a loyal member of one or more of these groups without impugning one's loyalty to the others", I said.

"Yes", said JFK, "even when some of these groups profess to be absolutely opposed to the others, one finds their officials working together behind the scenes in complete amity."

"You must be saying that supposedly different political factions have a great deal in common."

"Of course they do", said JFK, "especially when you consider that they have the same origins. Let us take the historic struggle between capitalism and communism, which is theoretically the shaping force of the twentieth century. What do we find? We find that Marx proposed to make capitalism more efficient by reducing the worker to a faceless zero, and that capitalism, while pretending to abhor the idea, enthusiastically accepted it. What sort of a struggle is that?"

"It is odd that people are not more aware of these similarities", I said.

"You must remember that the great advance in communications has drowned intelligence in information", said JFK. "People are no longer able to think, because they have all the facts. The groups have adopted similar techniques of mass communications, so and these techniques have influenced their ideas, so that they have become more or less interchangeable. It was then that the groups mounted their attack upon all of the factors from which they had derived their initial strength. Not the least of these factors was individual integrity. As a result, these groups have done everything within their power to destroy this integrity. They have persuaded the individual to join them by using the oldest formula known on earth for the enslavement of the individual."

"What is that?" I asked.

"The promise of freedom", said JFK. "Look around you and ask yourself, 'who is free.' Life is a series of obligations which chain down the individuals, the organism itself commits the individual to certain processes which he must repeat every day of his life. Nevertheless, the individual can develop within himself a knowledge of his own worth, a freedom of his own creation. It is this self-knowledge which the groups seek to destroy, and to substitute in its place the inner slavery of mass man, that is, man who has lost his individuality and his self-respect. This mass existence in turn opens the door to all sorts of outrages, not the least of which is man's determined onslaught against his own environment, which must inevitably culminate in his self-destruction. The groups introduce this concept of inner slavery in the individual by pretending to 'aid' or 'free' him, and they promote immorality, discord and all forms of criminal behavior. The purpose of this campaign on the part of the groups is to prove to everyone that the individual is immoral and irresponsible, and only the group can act to save the morality of mankind."

"Then it is your contention that the groups are the sponsors of the present day increase in crime and immorality?"

"There is no doubt about it", said JFK. "You can see the evidence on every hand. The groups have acted in concert to break down every legal restraint upon the individual, even in the act of murder, so that they can carry out their slogan of 'all power to the pluralist groups'."

"It seems rather paradoxical that the groups should seek to gain greater power by granting more freedom and license to the individuals, as well as by encouraging them in immorality", I said. "I should think that this would give the individual more power, and the groups less."

"Not at all", said JFK. "What this campaign is doing is lessening the restraints of conventional institutions on the individual, such as established law enforcement procedures, and setting up the pluralist groups as the only arbiters of right and wrong. Laws are ignored while the groups decide who shall be punished and who shall not. In other words, the groups are usurping power over the people by sweeping aside all traditional codes of behavior and laws, and they are setting up their own codes. This means that they are establishing their own sovereignty over the people. Eventually, by this means, their goal, 'all power to the pluralist groups' will be attained."

"That slogan sounds suspiciously like the banner of the Bolshevik Revolution in Russia", I said. "Wasn't that slogan, 'All power to the soviets'?"

"It certainly was", said JFK, "but you have no reason to wonder why the slogan of the pluralist groups should sound like it. As far as the fate of the individual is concerned, the pluralist groups and the Bolsheviks are the same types of people, who seek power by the same means."

"But the Bolsheviks are the bitter enemies of many groups in Russia", I said. "They fought the government departments, religious groups, in fact, they seemed to be against all groups."

"They were the bitter enemies of all groups which stood in their way", said JFK. "They destroyed all of the dissenting groups, one by one, even those which professed the same goals in the Revolution. The fate of the Mensheviks in Russia is much like the fate of those groups in the modern world which have resisted the pluralist society. They too have gone the way of the Mensheviks."

"It's too bad you didn't know all this when you were in the White House", I said. "Perhaps you could have done something about it."

"Too bad indeed", said JFK. "I would probably have been assassinated much sooner if I had had any idea of what was really going on."

"Do you mean that the pluralists had something to do with your assassination?" I asked.

"Yes, indeed", said JFK, "but that is a long and involved story, and I don't have time to go into it now. In fact, I don't have time to go into anything else just now, because the things we have to cover next must be developed in another conversation."

"Will it necessary for me to drive to Lyndhurst for our next conversation?" I asked.

"It isn't necessary", said JFK. "I can come here just as easily."

"Should I be alone?" I asked.

"That doesn't pose any problem", he said. "I thought it would be best today because I didn't want to surprise you here. As far as everyone else is concerned, if I come here again, you will seem to be resting quietly."

"Very well", I said. The radiance faded, and I heard my mother's quick firm step on the porch.

"You're having a lazy morning", she said. "You might as well have gone to church with me."

"I suppose so", I said. "I didn't get much accomplished here."

CONVERSATION THREE

Several weeks after my second conversation with John F. Kennedy, I still had done nothing about transcribing his words. On several occasions, I sat down to do so, poised myself at the typewriter, closed my eyes, and began to read the lines. Each time, I became so absorbed in the reading that I forgot all about typing them, and at the conclusion of the reading, I was both exhilarated and dejected by much that had been said.

Then too, there was the possibility that the time was not yet ripe, an excuse for postponement which I found most agreeable. After all, I told myself, these conversations are somewhat pessimistic in their overall content, even though they do offer a kind of hope to mankind. Would it not be more appropriate if I waited until things got worse for the majority of humanity, and thus more receptive to a philosophy which called for the exercise of much greater responsibilities on their part?

This was a comfortable summation, which allowed me as much time as I might choose, before I settled down to the serious work of transcribing the conversations, and the even more serious work of getting them into circulation. I had no illusions about the problems I would face here, since the conversations seemed to come no ready marketable category. Despite the observations on religion which they contained, they could hardly be said to be a religious dialogue. Nor were they political, even though the chief protagonist had been know chiefly on earth as a politician. They could simply described as literary in nature, and from the point of view, John F. Kennedy had chosen an unfortunate time to circulate his admonitions to mankind. Literature was no longer a marketable commodity. After having undergone a progressive sea-change from Chaucer to Shakespeare to Sir Walter Scott to James M. Cain, it had been knocked out of the ring by a new commodity called television. With his power of manifesting himself, it seemed to me that John F. Kennedy would have chosen one or all of the networks to present his evaluation of humanity's chances. Certainly he had used television before, with telling effect.

On second thought, I could understand that John F. Kennedy could not hope to convince anyone by such an appearance. A few old ladies would have heart attacks, men would become temporarily or permanently deranged, others would find the occasion an ideal one for robbing banks or paying off old scores, and in the end, an international panel of celebrated doctors would dismiss the event as an outstanding example of mass hallucination. The written word was still the only way in which to reach the sensible range of humanity. Despite the inevitable attempts to distort or dispel his conclusions, John F. Kennedy's words would ultimately have their effect.

Having reached this decision, I found it easy to put the conversations out of my mind. I continued to work hard at my insurance report business, and, as I periodically did, I made a trip to Richmond for one of the firms. I completed a number of reports in Waynesboro, and then drove on to Charlottesville. After interviewing some students there, I went to Richmond. This is a city which has always seemed peculiarly depressing, because of the sense of loss which hangs perceptibly over it. It is not so much the defeat of the Confederate cause which gives Richmond this dreary air, although it was here that the Confederacy made its last stand. Rather, it is the aura of silent mourning for the loss of everything which the founders of the nation held dear, and which is symbolized here by the seemingly permanent reign of the Byrd machine. Here the key members of the Byrd Organization drink themselves into insensibility, night after night, behind their locked doors, as they postpone the inevitable drying-out trip to Dejarnette's Sanatorium at Staunton, Va, which the Organization had built primarily to fill this ever-recurring need. These elderly, white-haired gentlemen, as interchangeable in makeup as boxes of National Biscuit Company soda crackers, did not drink so devotedly because they mourned the demise of the great democracy built on this site by Madison and Jefferson, nor did they drink because they were its undertakers. They drank simply because their lives were so damned dull. One could say of Richmond what the drummers used to say in Philadelphia, "I was there last week but it was closed."

Concluding my business in Richmond, I drove towards Washington. On the way, I stopped off for my usual visit to the battleground of the Wilderness, a few miles from Fredericksburg. The great peace and the tremendous sadness which pervades this field never fails to overcome me.

Few visitors stop there, and on this occasion, as on many previous ones, I did not see a living soul during the half hour that I wandered over the ridges and through the ravines. This isolation would seem to be the ideal spot for JFK to make another of his appearances, but he failed to materialize. I stooped to look closely at the odd mushrooms which grow thickly on this field, a yellow plant heavily flecked with red as though someone had bled profusely on it. Once again I established my rapport with the Confederate dead, the thousands of brave men whose bodies lie here. There are many other places in Virginia where the silent voices of history speak, but none where they seem so compelling.

I arrived in Alexandria in the early afternoon, several hours before I would meet the friends with whom I planned to stay. As had been my custom on previous visits, I decided to stop by Arlington Cemetery, and perhaps to visit the grave of John F. Kennedy. Although I had often driven through Arlington Cemetery, I usually stropped along the way to read the inscriptions on monuments to many of the brave men who, although their names do not appear in the history books, contributed much to the pacification of America. On these occasions, I wished to the victim of that tragic day in 1963, but had found it impossible because of the great number of people who had the same desire.

Today proved to be no different. I could see that a long line of visitors was waiting patiently for their turn to pause by the graveside. Perhaps I could wait in the car for awhile, until the crows swindled away. I parked the Buick in a convenient place along the road, and settled down in the car. The line winding towards the grave, rather than decreasing, seemed to be growing longer, but I hardly cared. I was at peace with the world, experiencing the great contentment which always came over me after I had visited the battlefield of the Wilderness. Being in Arlington seemed to intensify this feeling, and I had resolved long ago that, as a veteran, I would exercise my right to be buried here.

Once again I was engulfed by the radiance, as I entered the Presence of John F. Kennedy.

"Did you think you would have a better chance of finding me here?" he asked.

"My stopping here seemed to be accidental", I said, "although I hardly know whether anything is accidental any more. It's very peaceful here. Do you spend much time in Arlington?"

"No", replied JFK, "there isn't much I can do from here."

"I've been thinking a lot about the subject of our last conversation", I said. "It seems to me that if the groups and institutions which make up the pluralist consensus are as powerful as you say, that is even more reason why I would not have the slightest chance of putting your ideas into circulation."

"They're powerful, of course", said JFK. "I'm not denying that, but I do want to explain that they are only powerful in earthly power, and this is one of the weakest powers in the universe. You see, the very fact which dictated the choice of the earth as a fit place to settle exiles and criminals was the fact that it engenders a very low grade of power. This meant that the criminals would never be able to generate weapons which would be sufficiently powerful to threaten any other part of the universe. For instance, these pluralist groups seem to you to be very powerful, yet the fact is that they have no power at all except their hypnotic influence over mankind. They are materialist in nature, which simply means that their power is the low grade of earth material, and it would have no effect anywhere else. In fact, their power is of such a low grade that even a small group of individuals could end their influence overnight. It is for this reason that they are so quick to sense the opposition of anyone who refuses to accept their dogma in its entirety, and why they immediately act in concert to crush the slightest hint of rebellion against them. This too has a degrading influence upon all of earth, since it serves to hold back man's development. You must remember that earth power, or the impression of power, being of a low grade, can be shifted easily. When individuals hold power, of course it is likely to shift much more rapidly, and the effect of the pluralist groups has been to freeze power, or to attempt to hold it static in the forms into which they have diverted it. All of this is having an unfortunate effect upon the life of the individual, and, as I have pointed out before, it is aggravating all of the problems which face mankind."

"But how can the pluralist groups continue to aggravate these problems, without eventually being overcome by them?" I asked.

"They have been very adroit in manipulating these problems to their own advantage", said JFK, "but now they are being denied their principal instrument, war. Although wars may continue to be fought on a small scale, far from the great urban centers, as in Viet Nam, they can no longer be used to settle international differences, because they cannot be carried to a conclusion without abandoning conventional weapons. Sooner or later, one side of the other would yield to the temptation to use atomic weapons, especially if it were losing the war, and the result would devastate most of the world."

"But this atomic debacle is inevitable, anyway, isn't it?" I asked.

"Everything is inevitable", said JFK, "but that doesn't mean that it has to happen, or should be allowed to happen, now. What I am trying to say is that the pluralist groups have no means to solve or even to divert the tremendous problems which face them, and which, in the main, they have created. This opens the way for individuals to move in and regain some of the power, by offering solutions to these problems. This would serve to curb the power of the pluralists."

"You mentioned that the capacity of the individual for good was almost unlimited, and that the capacity of the group for evil was also almost unlimited. In view of what you have told me about the origin of life on earth as a place of exile or punishment for misfits and criminals from other modes of being, it seems to me that it would be the other way around? Why wouldn't the groups be organized to use their combined forces for good, as many of them claim, and to restrain the irresponsibility and evil impulses of the individual?"

"That's a very logical question, and one which I had intended to answer in our last conversation. Most of the pluralist groups do have noble aims. Their stated goals are models of what is known as 'doing good'. However one of the great errors of mankind is that they tend to accept goals as fait accompli. They seem incapable of realizing just what the pluralist groups are doing, but if these results are examined closely and impartially, it can be seen that everything they do has an evil consequence. For instance, nearly all of these groups promote universal education, which, on the surface, is a praiseworthy aim. And yet, what do we find when we examine the results of this work. We see that the pluralists are merely conditioning the people to receive information, and that this is information is in nearly every instance propaganda of the most blatant kind, which the people are not in a position to challenge. This propaganda, of course, is always intended to serve one or more of the pluralist goals. At the same time, these groups are attacking individuality by destroying the ability of the individual to think for himself. For instance, during the so-called Dark Ages, when the vast majority of the world's population was illiterate, do you suppose that men were incapable of judging things, or of making an intelligent choice? I have already pointed out that the large universities spend billions of dollars each year, without producing a single scholar who is capable of independently pursuing a course of research or of formulating his personal theories. Present day philosophy consists of pouring from one empty vessel into another, while the students dare not point out that there are no contents in either one."

"It seems to me that the academic philosophers have developed a private language", I said, "from which the rest of the world is excluded."

"It is a private language consisting solely of doubletalk", said JFK, "which is intended only to prevent the rest of the world from discovering that the philosophers have nothing to say."

"Is that why men like Albert Schweitzer fled the great academic centers of Europe" I asked, "preferring to spend their lives in the wilderness?"

"Schweitzer knew that if he was to continue to live, he had to go where there was life", said JFK. "Europe had become an intellectual graveyard, and he had no wish to be buried alive. This, of course, is the fate of all who enter the universities. There is plenty of money for all this, but the money is only the dirt which is thrown in on top of the coffin, to ensure that the corpse will not be able to dig its way out, even if it should recover consciousness. There are thousands of people who are studying on fellowships, but these are only paid vacations where it is expected that the scholar will do as little as possible. Many of them, indeed, specify that he is to produce nothing — he is only to meditate! This, of course, is the unspoken purpose behind all of them. They are encouraged to focus their intellectual energies upon any topic that is far removed from the realities of everyday life — for instance, the sex life of the tumbleweed. In no case are they allowed to examine the problems of mankind which the pluralists have created and aggravated. It's no secret that the quality of education is tobogganing downhill, and the ones who are most resentful of this are naturally, those who suffer most from it — the students. I'm not exaggerating when I say that the education which I obtained at

Harvard a couple of decades ago was three times as good as the instruction you get there today."

"That certainly creates a confusing situation", I said. "How am I expected to convince people that all of these organizations which ostensibly are set up to improve the lot of mankind are actually the source of most of their troubles?"

"You can't convince anyone of anything", said JFK. "You have to force them to look for themselves. You must awaken the sleeping masses!"

"I begin to think that everything on earth is paradoxical", I said.

"From the universal view", said JFK, "everything on earth can be seen to operate in two ways, both forwards and backwards, for itself and against itself. This is a necessary process, for those elements which have no external opposition to allow them to stand upright must manufacture their own internal opposition. Thus good seems to be bad; bad seems to be good. Then too, man's origins are essentially evil, as the ancient doctrine of original sin implies; that is, he is a flawed creature, who is as likely to do evil as to do good. Yet the life of the individual becomes an exercise in good, even though it begins from a premise of evil. In the same way, the work of the pluralist groups, which are supposedly designed as exercises in good, become works of evil."

"Why is that?" I asked.

"By seeking to oppose or to replace the individual in every walk of life", said JFK, "the pluralist groups are working against the fundamental purpose of life on earth. You see, every individual human is in some way working out a problem on earth, an exercise in good and evil, and the nature of these problems is never identical."

"Do you mean that there are at present more than two billion problems, or exercises in good and evil, being worked out on earth?" I asked.

"You can say that", replied JFK, "or you can say that there are two billion aspects of the same problem now in process. It is like saying that everything is the same, and yet everything is different."

"If this is part of the universal plan", I said, "it would seem that man leads an essentially religious existence."

"Men, animals, and also plants play their role in this ecology of the universe", said JFK, "and in this respect, it could be said to be a religious existence."

"Is that why religious leaders are attempting to play a more direct role in everyday life?" I asked.

"The function of religion is to appeal to man's higher nature", said JFK. "You might say that it is the old differentiation between the mud and the stars. Religion is primarily a thing of the stars, intended to remind man that he is not bound forever to the earth. It is only when religion abandons this role and descends into the mud, so to speak, miring itself in the daily mechanics of life on earth, that it loses its power over the minds of men."

"Isn't this a criticism of much religious activity today?" I asked. "Aren't you saying that social action is not a proper function of religion?"

"Everything in the universe", said JFK, "waxes and wanes. It waxes when it is true to its own precepts, its original premises, and it wanes when it is attracted away from them by other forces."

"When you say that everyone on earth is working out a problem through his own destiny, is that a contradiction of determinism, or is it a confirmation of it?"

"It is neither", said JFK. "Determinism is the impersonal sweep of personal forces, and it is also the personal sweep of impersonal forces. The universe has not determined that you will have chicken for lunch a 1:00 on Tuesday, but it may afterwards seem to you that it was inevitable. Determinism is simply this: things must and do happen. The universe is not static or frozen, even though vast areas of it may seem to be. It may seem motionless only because we are unable to see what is in motion, or it may be beyond our powers to see what is in motion. One of the flaws of individual choice is the refusal to let things happen, to place oneself in the way of events rather than to take part in them. This occurs because the individual has faulty preconceptions of what is good and what is evil. Things are not determined in a particular pattern, either for good or for evil, but are designed to accommodate both. Everything which occurs takes place within the laws of the system, and from that standpoint, the universe is determinist. However, within the system, things are not determinist, and a great deal of choice is exercised. Much of this choice is dictated by the desire for survival; some of it may be classified as the operation of moral choice, or a conscious resolution for good or for evil. Although these decisions are made in a determinist system, they are non-determinist in themselves. But, since each of these decisions or acts affects all of the other decisions or acts which are taking place, and inasmuch as a decision or act is affected by all of the other decisions or acts over which it has no control, then this would be determinist."

"The more you explain, the less I understand", I said.

"Then you have some idea of the magnitude of your task", said JFK. "You can see why Christ spoke in parables. You must do whatever is necessary to get the message across. No matter how you do it, however, you must always remember that the most confusing thing about the universe is its utter simplicity. Your main problem in communicating with others is to prevent them from transforming this simplicity into meaningless complexities. Man has always been trained to look for things which are not there, and which have never existed, to seek causes and effects which are entirely imaginary. The process of education is designed to prevent man from understanding himself and the universe. One of the greatest strides in this direction was the development of professional, or vocational 'education'."

"But civilization is built entirely upon vocational and professional education", I protested. "Without it, we would be no more advanced than the African pygmies."

"And even with it, we are no more advanced than the African pygmies", said JF. "You see, everyone must receive two complete courses of education if he is to fulfill his role in life and to work out his personal problem in the universal destiny. He must have the professional or vocational training which will enable him to play a useful role in society, and he must also be educated to understand himself, to think for himself, and to understand others. This is primarily a religious education, since it involves man's higher nature, and without it, a man is still a barbarian, no matter what position he manages to attain in life. Ha may be the president of a university or a world-famous artist, but if his higher nature has not been educated, he is no more civilized than an Australian aborigine. In fact, he is less, because the primitive societies always undertake some education in man's relation to nature and the universe. Not even a savage would believe that we come from nothing and are headed toward nothing, which is the personal philosophy, or Nihilism, of the leaders of the pluralist groups."

"I should think that they would be paralyzed by such a belief", I said. "How could a man carry on professional work with such an attitude towards himself and others?"

"He can do it because he is an educated savage", said JFK, "that is, a barbarian who has been trained to accept anything. One finds these Nihilists in every walk of life, in education, in religion, in politics. These people are the most typical products of modern education. They are the successful graduates of the mechanist school of thought, the artificially developed attitude which can best be summed up as toilet training."

"But toilet training is one of the essentials of taking one's place as a civilized being", I said.

"Exactly", said JFK. "Toilet training exemplifies the transformation from a semi-helpless child who must be looked after constantly, to a semi-adult who can control his actions and live with others without offending them. The point I am trying to make is that toilet training, an essential part of education, has become the end-all of education, and that development of the mind, the primary basis of education, is now ignored."

"To put it bluntly, you mean that the product of modern education can control his sphincter muscle, but he has an irresponsible mind", I said.

"That is the underlying situation of many present day problems", said JFK. "That is why Freud was so interested in toilet training. Recognizing it as a milestone in the development of the individual, he was overwhelmed by his own discovery, and he came to the conclusion that it was the most important such step. It was inevitable that those who came after him, and who elaborated on his theories, should have carried them out in actual life, producing the sort of human absurdities who now direct the activities of the pluralist groups. You see, toilet training, or the Pavlovian conditioning of the muscles to certain processes of impulse, control and response, is purely mechanistic, and is on a different level from man's role as an intelligent being. Yet mechanically trained individuals are now hailed everywhere as the true intellectuals, the arbiters of man's art of living. The professional man whose mind remains undeveloped is no more admirable, and no more worthy of emulation, than a skilled bricklayer of carpenter, yet we do not allow bricklayers or carpenters to lead political parties, art associations, or develop educational theories. The only professional worthy of admiration, or deserving leadership, is one who has contributed some original thought to mankind. This was the purpose of the thesis which was required to become a doctor of philosophy, and it is for this reason that all graduate work requires a thesis of some kind. As the mechanically trained people gradually replaced the humanist educators, these requirements were watered down so as to become meaningless, in order to allow the products of the toilet training school to achieve leadership in all of the humanist endeavours."

"Then you consider the mechanically trained people to have untrained minds?" I asked.

"They are completely irresponsible", said JFK, "which amounts to the same thing, and they exhibit this irresponsibility at every opportunity. One sees university presidents encouraging the students to riot and to lead immoral lives; judges encouraging criminals to resume their lives of crime by freeing them, and doctors who do not hesitate to prescribe drugs for patients which endanger their lives."

"Is this what is meant by 'the failure of nerve'?" I asked.

"It isn't a failure", said JFK, "it is the inevitable result of neglect, of good human minds gone to seed."

"I suppose that is why a few moralists are crying out against the immorality and the anarchy or our time" I said.

"It isn't immorality or anarchy", said JFK, "it is simply the tragic spectacle of life taking a wrong turn, and going down a blind alley. One of the great crimes against mankind was the substitution of this toilet training for the development of the human mind, and by replacing the life of the mind by this mechanical technique of daily living. It is this, as much as anything else, which has hypnotized mankind and put him into an unnatural sleep. It is as though a huge pendulum, Poe's pendulum, if you will, had been swinging and swinging over the man who is on the brink of the pit, and as though its mechanical action had finally hypnotized him to the point where he was no longer concerned about his imminent end.

This is the true state of mankind today. There have been long eras in the past, of course, when man entered upon long periods of sleep, even while he was carrying on ostensible life and even building great civilizations. These were either the creations of a few minds which were alive, and who directed the sleepwalkers, or the entire development was the product of generations who where asleep."

"Then civilization can be developed by men who are not fully conscious?" I asked.

"All of them have been", said JFK. "I was unfortunate that despite his vast researches, Spengler was unable to discern this simple fact. It would have answered most of his questions. However, no previous civilization has existed on the brink of universal, or rather, earthly, destruction, as does this one. It is quite dangerous for sleepwalkers to be roaming about, carrying loaded guns which they may fire at any time."

"Then you consider that mechanical education induces a state of hypnosis in man?" I asked.

"The kind of life which is produced by the products of mechanical education is hypnotic", said JFK. "It induces sleep by the simple factor of endless repetition. Sleep is also induced by the great sense of emptiness, of wandering forever across an endless landscape. As the poet wrote,

> *'And when the mourners, spent in their perfect war,*
> *turned in the light like figurines, amber in the amber light,*
> *and the cortege, on the treadmill of its own exhaustion,*
> *marched forever across the frozen scene'"*

"It seems quite depressing", I said.

"Depressing, and exhausting", said JFK, "but life always waits patiently for the thrilling moment of life, even if it has to wait forever. The poet has described that for us,

> *'Let the thought of a breeze or shadow touch, tremble the object. Immediately like an echo built-in by daedalian extravagance, steel-and-concrete throats burst into song, dried blood opened like caked starch, the pelting music rang on the ice.'"*

"I can understand why the mechanical way of life is exhausting", I said, "when man is condemned to repeat the same limited motions throughout his life, in a world which has become a huge factory."

"It is also wasteful", said JFK. "Think of the expenditure when adult human beings spend six or eight years of their life in repetitious toilet training to become semi-educated doctors and engineers. We can hardly blame the university students for becoming bored and resentful."

"But you can hardly dismiss such highly technical subjects as engineering, medicine or law by calling them 'toilet training'!" I exclaimed.

"Basically, they are the same", said JFK. "They are exercises in mechanical aptitudes and conditioned responses. For instance, the doctors takes a temperature. He is trained to respond in different ways to different numbers. He traces a pain in the body by its physical course, and he relies heavily upon various mechanical devices, such the X-ray, for his diagnosis and treatment. The engineer's work, of course, is purely mechanical, being based upon stresses and strains. The study of law presumes that one will master a set of artificial and mechanical rules which direct the commercial and community life of man. If one really follows the law, human intelligence plays no part in a lawyer's life. If he exercises his own mind, he is judged guilty of a legal error. None of these professions train a man's intelligence or expect him to use it. Even my father's profession, that of financier, was a mechanical one. It was his job to examine a situation, determine how much money would be needed to control it, whether there was a market for it, and the margin of profit. The more mechanical his method, the more likely his success. He concentrated on this sort of thing early in life, and he became very good at it. As he once said, a really good banker has no human factor to consider. He could estimate the value of a situation with the rapidity of a computer, and he never allowed his emotions to influence his decisions. I think he could have given an exact estimate of my value, or of any of my brothers, at any time."

"Is there a connection between the mechanical nature of the professions and the nature of the pluralist groups?" I asked.

"There is a great deal of connection", said JFK. "In fact, the tremendous increase in the power of the pluralist groups is due to the fact that they have built their strength around the mechanist professional class. Because the professionals have undergone a longer period of training, or conditioned response, they are more easily controlled, and they are also more sympathetic to existing in a pluralist society. Consequently, they have become the backbone of the pluralist groups. Educationists, bankers, doctors, lawyers, all have enthusiastically adopted the doctrines of pluralism, because their own short-term goals of becoming associated with some sort of institution in order to receive a comfortable lifetime income sort of institution with the pluralist technique of controlling mankind through institutions."

"Would you say that the relatively uneducated working people are the most individualistic?" I asked.

"Of course they are", said JFK, "because they have not been trained for as long a time in the conditioned response. Unfortunately, they do not realize this, and throughout their lives, they accept and are hypnotized by the mechanical movements of the professional class. Even though they have not received the same amount of toilet trained, the working people are controlled by it because they allow the so-called educated class to make the decisions. In their inner being, those individuals who have only received a grammar school or high school education realize that they still retain certain powers which the educated classes have lost, but they do not know what to do with them, one might describe this precious quality as their intellectual virtue, or innocence. Despite their knowledge of this quality within themselves, they acknowledge the educated group as a superior class."

"Why is this?" I asked.

"The reason is quite simple", said JFK. "and rather surprising. The less-educated individual respects the professional man simply because the professional uses good grammar. During their lengthy and extended period of toilet training, which lasts long into their adult lives, the professionals are compelled to express themselves according to the rules of mechanical educationists. This is based upon the use of proper sentences and in general, employing a somewhat more extensive vocabulary than that daily used by the less-educated groups. When the professionals emerge into community life, this 'good grammar' becomes an identifying sign, a sort of jargon which sets them apart from the less-educated people. By the use of proper grammar and their vocabulary, the professional class, on a superficial level, appears to be more intelligent than the working people, even though the less-educated are actually more adept in using their minds and in understanding new situations."

"Are you referring to what is called 'peasant shrewdness'?" I asked.

"One might call it the resourcefulness of a mind which had not been ruined", said JFK. "This difference is quite marked in warfare, when the most satisfactory infantryman, who is often alone in the field and must rely on his own decisions, is found to be a farm boy with little formal education. The mechanically trained professional class remains at command posts to garble the information sent back to them and order patrols into the wrong areas, where they are wiped out. This is the officer class."

"I hope it wasn't some mechanically trained professional who sent your PT boat careening into that Japanese destroyer", I said.

"You could say that that was amateur night", said JFK.

"Then it is you contention that the professional officer wastes the lives of intelligent infantrymen?" I asked.

"Not from any conscious resolve to do so", said JFK. "However, officers are usually aware that one of the purposes of war is to use up as many lives as possible. A commander who never lost any men would become an object of deep suspicion to his follow officers. It is usually civilian commanders like Ethan Allen who win engagements without losing a man."

"Now that I'm aware of it", I said, "I'm glad that I'm no longer in the army."

"The mention of war brings up the principal undercurrent which directs and informs all life on earth", said JFK.

"What undercurrent is that?" I asked.

"The pathological force", said JFK, "or, if you prefer, the force of evil."

"Then it is your understanding, from where you now observe life on earth, that the primary direction of life is evil?" I asked.

"There's no reason to put yourself in my position just to observe that", said JFK. "It should be quite obvious to anyone."

"But you never commented on it while you were living on earth, did you?"

"No, I did not. You see, I wasn't thinking in those terms. However, I can now see quite clearly that the great directing force in the development of life on earth has always been war, famine and pestilence."

"Do you mean that man is what he is today because of these things, rather than because of the goodwill of a benevolent God?" I asked.

"It ought to be plain that every biological mutation or adaptation of man has been caused by elements which malevolently altered or threatened the very nature of man", said JFK.

"But the Black Plague, which endangered the population of Europe, caused no significant change in man's system", I said.

"Are you certain of that?" asked JFK. "Remember, there have been no recurrences. Doesn't that argue that man, or those who survived, developed a mode of resisting this plague?"

"It's possible", I said. "Certainly there was no vaccination or other medical remedy to prevent it."

"At any rate, it was a virus", said JFK, "and viruses do not usually cause significant changes in man, because the human organism is not geared to adapt itself to such a quick or virulent onslaught, or to alter its makeup in time to prepare an adequate defense. No, I was referring to the development of man from his earliest origins on earth, when he existed as a one-celled organism long before the moon split away and caused great cataclysmic changes in all of the forms of life. That period of one-celled life, incidentally, was man's Golden Age, a time which he remembers nostalgically when existence was quite simple and pleasurable, since these one-celled organisms lived in an environment which provided them adequate sustenance without effort on their part. This was life in the Enchanted Isles, of which man has a very dim but very pleasant memory, for the simple reason that the organism lived a placid and undisturbed existence. It was much later, when the earth underwent severe changes, and life had to devise more and more devious methods of surviving and maintaining itself, that other parts of the universe recognized this adaptability, and realized that this would be a convenient dumping-ground for its their misfits and criminals."

"Then you are able to descry no benevolent influence in the development of man?" I asked.

"I didn't say that", replied JFK. "I simply pointed out that the major modifications in man's makeup had been caused by the challenge of factors which in themselves were far from benevolent."

"But there is a deep purpose behind all of this", I said. "Isn't this the legendary Calvary of man?"

"There's no question that a certain amount of suffering is an integral part of every man's destiny", said JFK. "It is also known that this quantity of suffering is intended to materially influence him in his attitudes towards himself, his life and his fellow-beings. How he reacts to the impact of this suffering is an essential element in the manner in which he works out his problem during his time on earth."

"Then the earth really is a Dante's Inferno", I said, "in which the tormented ones eternally work out their Sisyphean tasks."

"Not eternally", said JFK, "and not Sisyphean. That is one blessing of life on earth, that it is limited, and our tasks seem to be endless and meaningless only because we cannot discern their end and do not understand their meaning. In every aspect of the earth's ecology, there is a great proportion of illogic, frustration and insanity."

"We're certainly able to discern that", I said. "We have only to observe President Johnson signing orders for billion-dollar expenditures in other lands, as he sits in the White House surrounded by miles of stinking slums."

"I hope you're not trying to remind me that those slums were also there while I was President", said JFK. "After all, I signed quite a few billion dollar appropriations."

"I didn't mean it as a personal criticism either of you or of Lyndon Johnson", I said. "I was only trying to point out that the paradoxes of modern life, and especially in America, can only be described as insane."

"As far as those slums are concerned, you might remember that the inability to see what is closest to us, or the ability to shut it out, is one of the features of life's limited consciousness.

Besides, we have never been lucky enough to find a foreign power who was willing to come over and bomb our slums for us. You might also remember that in order to remain habitable, cities should be rebuilt every hundred years. It helps if they are razed to the ground. As a matter of fact, most of the slums in Washington are less than a hundred years old."

"Could you say that these slums are an indictment of capitalism?" I asked.

"They are principally an indictment of the people who live in them", said JFK. "Slums are a characteristic of most large cities throughout the world, whether they are located in capitalistic countries or not. Slums appear when the people who live in buildings or the people who own them do not bother to maintain them in a habitable condition."

"Aren't most slums inhabited by people who rent?" I asked. "That is a black eye for capitalism."

"Slums are profitable", said JFK, "but that is not necessarily an indictment of the profit system. What is needed is a program of slum rehabilitation which will still make it profitable for someone to own and maintain them."

"Since we seem to have gotten in rather deep on such a variety of subjects, I'm beginning to wonder how long you expect to continue this series of conversations", I said.

"This is the third one, and it should be the last", said JFK. "I can see no reason why we should have to develop any of these subjects any further. I've covered the material that I wanted you to transcribe, and we've gone into things about as much as we can without getting so involved that it would be far beyond any potential audience's ability to assimilate. We also have the problem of becoming too esoteric in pursuing these subjects, and of encountering an impossible wall of disbelief."

"Disbelief is about the only reaction that I'm anticipating", I said.

"The fact that such an important step is taking place, and that the curtain is being lifted, although only a little, would certainly cause disbelief", said JFK. "This is because a mechanically-trained population expects an easily discernible cause and effect. You will have the problem of finding an answer for the inevitable question of why you are doing this, or that great comeback of mankind, 'what's in it for you?'"

"I'm glad you raised that question", I said, "although I won't say I would have brought it up myself. Just what is in all this for me?"

"Just what's in life for anyone", said JFK. "The fact that the curtain has been lifted, and only a little, means that it was of great importance for all mankind that this be done, and done now. So you will get out of it just what anyone else gets out of it."

"Can this reward be put in a few words?" I asked.

"Man must be reminded of his own nature", said JFK, "if he is to survive. He must become aware of his quest for self-realization, and such freedom as he can hope to achieve on earth."

"From what you have said about the power of the pluralists", I said, "that doesn't seem to be much of an offer of freedom."

"Enslavement by the pluralists is not the real danger", said JFK, "although it is a real one. Their kind of slavery is only a surface one, since it is a mechanical process. Because of the peculiar strictures placed upon him by his origins, the nature of his existence, and his mission on earth, man will never attain any sort of the freedom which is noised about as his future. You may as well make it clear that the inhabitants of earth will never reach the day when all of their responsibilities will be suddenly lifted from them, so that they can wander about, enjoying life, travelling from country to country without a care as to family life, labor, or personal destiny. What man must realize is that even though he has no chance of ever realizing that kind of freedom, or irresponsibility, he does have a choice as to the kind of service he will undertake during his lifetime."

"By service, I suppose you mean bondage", I said.

"It is bondage inasmuch as men id bound to certain tasks which he cannot evade", said JFK. "For instance, how much freedom do you think that I enjoyed during my life on earth?"

"I would have thought that you had a great deal", I said. "With the vast fortune amassed by your father, you could have ignored many of the problems which enslaved your fellow men. I have already suggested that you could have followed the artistic career which was your only genuine ambition."

"That's a surprisingly conventional answer from someone who is supposed to be an artist", said JFK. "Have you had so little experience of life that you think wealthy people have no responsibilities?"

"I didn't say that", I replied. "I said that they could afford to follow the career of their own choice."

"As is true of everyone else, that depends upon what obligations they have", said JFK. "Do you really think I could have become a Harry Crosby or a Peggy Guggenheim, throwing costume parties year after year in the high-rent district in Paris? My desire to paint was a desire to work, but I couldn't follow it merely because it was an inner desire, or even a compulsion. A poor boy would have had much more chance to obey such a compulsion that I would. You see, my father had spent his entire life in accumulating a fortune for his family, and one of the use to which this fortune was to be put was the financing of our futures. It was expected that we would make our mark, and it was also expected that we would follow conventional financial lines. Art wouldn't have come in that category."

"Then it was a gift with strings attached", I said.

"It wasn't a gift, it was an instrument", said JFK, "an instrument which we were expected to put to the best possible use. This doesn't mean that we could not have ignored or bypassed some of those responsibilities, but our training made it virtually impossible that that would happen, and it didn't. I only mention this to explain to you the restrictions which bound every man's life. There are not only the responsibilities laid upon us by our necessity to fulfill our role for the family, race and nation, but there is also the further task of weaving one's small part in the vast tapestry of life which is being woven on the loom of the universe. In this, too, the earth is only a small segment."

"But the realization of this seems too much for mankind", I said. "How could one man's life retain any significance in such a vast scheme of things?"

"I thought I had covered all that in my emphasis upon the creative possibilities of the individual", said JFK. "If I have failed to get that across to you, I can see that you will have real problems in presenting it to mankind. Let me briefly recapitulate what has been said. Life transcends death, or rather, they are differing aspects of one process; man labors under the shadow of original sin, which our theologians have defined as the sin of the first man, or Adam, but which, of course, is really the sin of those who spawned life on earth; and mankind is now on the verge of destroying himself and the earth. One of the principal causes of this dangerous situation is the fact that man has lost sight of his own uniqueness, or originality of being, he has renounced his claim to his personal spark of divinity and he is rapidly surrendering to pluralist groups the last vestiges of his self-respect. This opens the doors to the pluralists and gives them their opportunity to aggravate all of the problems which now threaten the continued existence of earth. I pointed out that Jesus Christ offered the antidote to all this two thousand years ago, when he reminded man of his uniqueness in the sight of God, his individual values, and his mission."

"And how long do you think it would take to effect any sort of a reversal of the situation?" I asked.

"It will be a long and gradual process", said JFK. "It is possible that some of the pluralist forces would themselves be converted and would aid in spreading this warning. In the final analysis, however, the power of the pluralists, which has grown and manifested itself in an inhuman and mechanical manner, can be overcome by man's assertion of himself as a unique individual, as a being with his own right to existence, as a creature with the divine spark of the Godhead within him. He can facilitate this victory by asserting himself in Christ, and by throwing off the hypnotic and mechanist influence of the pluralist groups."

"How would you describe the situation of Christ at the present time?" I asked. "There have been some description of Him as an ascended master."

"That's as good description as any", said JFK, "sitting on the right hand of power, I believe he described it."

"And are you an ascended master?" I asked.

"Not for a long time", said JFK. "It doesn't come automatically with martyrdom, you know.

Perhaps I will be, if this task can be carried out successfully."

"And what if I make a complete botch of it?" I asked. "How will that affect you?"

"I may be allowed to try someone else", he said, "but it would be most likely that I would have to undertake a sojourn on earth. This would be much more difficult than what you are being asked to do, because once I had assumed another earthly body, I would have no conscious knowledge of my mission, and it would be a long and painstaking process before I arrived at that self-knowledge."

"Do you mean something akin to the regimen of a Yoga?" I asked.

"That is one way of doing it", said JFK. "Whatever the way, it would be a long and arduous process of preparation. The advantage in employing you is that you have already undergone quite a bit of that process."

"Do you mean the disappointments?" I asked. "Crowding five hundred years of disillusionment into a single decade?"

"Don't sell yourself short", advised JFK. "A lot more than five hundred years went into that. Of course, there are a couple of billion people on earth who would want to help in this, provided that it was properly explained to them. At any rate, that decision won't be left to me. You'll be given enough time to do what you can, and after that, other arrangements will be made."

"With an opportunity to do something on this scale, I should think you would welcome another sojourn on earth."

"No one ever welcomes another sojourn on earth", said JFK. "You see, once you have a clear view of what it's really like, it's not very comfortable on earth."

"Then this work will make it uncomfortable for everyone there."

"Not necessarily", said JFK. "Life on earth has all sorts of built-in safeguards against becoming too depressed about anything. It's one of the things that makes life there bearable."

"You are referring now to the pathological aspects of man's existence?"

"I mean the sheer malevolence of the animal nature, which, of course, springs full-blown from its origins. When Freud wrote of the psychopathology of everyday life, he was, as usual, skimming over the surface of reality, skipping stones across the pond of existence. He attached great importance to a slip of the tongue as a revelation of one person's subconscious hostility towards another, but he never dared to pry up the stone and look at the real forms which wriggled underneath. It never seemed to have occurred to him that all of the fundamental relationships between humans are conditioned by pathological desires so terrible that we cannot acknowledge them, and we must keep them hidden deep within our subconscious mind."

"That's a rather grim view, isn't it? What about love? What about family life? What about the communal efforts of people to help each other?"

"These things exist, certainly", said JFK, "and they too are an important part of man's life. But they are the visible part, the portion of the iceberg which rears above the water. That isn't the part which sinks the ships. I was merely commenting that Freud could not acknowledge to himself that the desire to abuse, enslave, torture and murder other human beings plays a major role in most human relationships. Even the sex act is a violation of one human being by another, but it is the only means of procreation afforded to man. Doesn't that give you some idea of the pathological basis of life on earth? What about the very act of parturition through which humans begin their earthly existence, as they burst into consciousness through a mist of blood and shame?"

"You are beginning to sound very existential", I said.

"Life is an existential matter", said JFK.

"What about the theory of natural law which was propounded by the Greeks?" I asked. "Didn't they decide that the concept of the physical world as the plaything of these dark powers was being offset by the emergence of an intelligent and logical order exhibiting first principles?"

"Indeed they did", said JFK, "and indeed it is. I hadn't expected to go this far with you, but since you have brought it up, I might as well explain that this is the real crux of the entire matter. Although it is an oversimplification to call the world a plaything of the dark powers, it is quite true that life on earth appeared as a result of evil in the universe, and of the decision by other modes of being to make the earth a place of exile and punishment for those elements which had been found too unfit or too pathological to maintain their natural place in their own environment. Once this had been done, the rest of the universe paid little attention to earth for a very long period of time. They finally realized that a kind of life had begun to appear on earth which was not completely dominated by the characteristics of the evil forms which had been exiled there. To put it plainly, good was beginning to appear from evil."

"And was this good form of life man?" I asked.

"Oh, no, this was eons before the appearance of man", said JFK. "This development was of tremendous interest to the rest of the universe of all worlds, I should say, but for conversational purposes it is simpler to refer only to this one, even though it is but an insignificant part."

"Then it is not possible elsewhere in the universe for good to appear from evil?" I asked.

"It had never been given the opportunity", explained JFK. "First of all, you must realize that life in other modes of being developed more directly, one might say, in a sort of straight line. The possibility of discontinuity has only appeared on earth."

"Do you have any prediction as to how much time the earth has left before its destruction becomes unavoidable?" I asked.

"That's difficult to say", replied JFK. "It could happen at any time. You see, there have already been two severe crises when atomic war was averted only by sheer luck, or so it seemed."

"I suppose you are referring to the Cuban crisis and the Berlin crisis", I said.

"No, I do not mean the Berlin crisis or the Cuban crisis", said JFK. "Those crises were never as serious as they were portrayed by the press. After all, the press, as the spokesman for the pluralist groups, deals primarily with crises of one kind, or another, both genuine and manufactured ones. Neither of these incidents ever got into the press, but it wouldn't be fair to people still living to discuss them."

"You're saying, then, that such a war could occur at any time?"

"A loaded gun can be fired at any time", said JFK, "Even if it has a good safety catch."

"You've certainly managed to interest me in this thing", I said, "even if you can't convince me that I have any chance of success. I only wish you could do more directly to help."

"The days when the gods hovered over the battlefield, aiding their personal favorites, ended long ago", said JFK.

"Do you mean there really was such a time?" I asked.

"There were many aspects of life which are no longer possible", said JFK, "just as there are many things now, which were not possible a few centuries ago."

"Then I understand that you are powerless to aid the success of this project", I said.

"Not powerless", said JFK. "It's simply that I am too far removed from it all."

"I have little confidence that I'll be able to accomplish what you hope from me", I said.

"That is because you have always failed in what you set out to do", said JFK.

"And your record is just the opposite", I replied. "You always succeeded in what you attempted."

"I usually attained my goal", said JFK. "However, the goal wasn't everything I had expected it to be. My success could be called an error on my part, if one could be said to make an error of which one knew nothing beforehand. I really believed that it would be possible to change things and still go along with the world."

"And it isn't possible?" I asked.

"Of course not", said JFK, "as you have always known. That's another reason why you were the only person who could be seriously considered for this task. You have always gone against the world."

"And the world has always won", I said.

"It has been a meaningful struggle", said JFK. "Have you ever stopped to think that you could have gone much further if you had compromised, if you had agreed to go along with the world, just a little."

"It occurred to me", I said.

"But you never did."

"No, I had that thought, and I had the opportunity, but I never did. I sometimes wondered why."

"My experience was quite different", said JFK. "I had always believed that you could go along with the world, as long as you retained sight of your own noble aspirations."

"Then you did have high aspirations?" I asked.

"Of course I did", said JFK. "It wasn't merely words. Why do you think the world welcomed me so enthusiastically? It wasn't because of my youth or energy, or that I was a golden lad from the golden west. It was because I was really offering the world something."

"And the world was eager for you", I said. "The world always welcomes someone whom it can corrupt. A man is merely another boy who has been destroyed."

"I walked into it", said JFK. "By the time I had gotten up to my ears in that pathological mess, Dallas wasn't as great a shock as it might have been. I won't deny that I was a sitting duck. After all, I had every benefit of a mechanical education at the hands of the pluralist groups."

"I had some education, too", I reminded him.

"But yours didn't take", said JFK. "Not one inoculation ever penetrated your hide, whereas I soaked it all up and asked for more."

"And that is you explanation for the fact that I have always gone against the world?" I asked.

"That's about it", said JFK.

"It doesn't make for much of a life", I said.

"It's all there is", said JFK. "Man's destiny is plain enough, after all of these centuries. Fight or die."

"And the dice are loaded", I said. "You're sure to die anyway."

"Yes, but if you refuse to fight, your life doesn't have any meaning", said JFK. "Man doesn't die because he gets old and feeble. He dies because he stops fighting. That's why the life of Christ is such a lesson for every man."

"Because He was crucified?" I asked.

"He walked the road to Calvary", said JFK, "and He was crucified. But He never gave one inch to the world, and so the world won, but the world lost because Christ showed for all time how a man must live his life, if it is to have any meaning."

"Hasn't anything changed?" I asked. "It's been two thousand years since Christ was crucified?"

"What has changed?" asked JFK. "The Pharisees can still summon the soldiers to arrest those who oppose them."

"I wish I could understand the plan behind it all", I said.

"But you do understand it", said JFK. "Every man has an instinctive understanding of the plan. One of the functions of life is to obscure that understanding, or to keep it tucked snugly away in the subconscious."

"You have made the point that one's life has no meaning if one refuses to fight", I said, "but from what you've had to say about it, it hardly seems worthwhile."

"It's worthwhile, all right", said JFK. "The very nature of life on earth is hellish, because the moment that conditions become completely favorable for life, that is the very moment that life becomes a menace to itself, outstripping its food supplies, devouring itself, turning against itself. This is the explanation of man's inner pathological nature. As soon as things begin to improve for him, his basic instincts order him to make them worse."

"Thant sounds like Poe's favorite subject, the Imp of the Perverse", I said.

"One could call it perversity", said JFK, "but it goes much deeper than that. Poe was aware that there was this satanic instinct in man, deep within his nature, the desire to hurt and destroy even when it was in direct contravention of his own interests. Poe never pursued the matter, but played with it in the usual nineteenth century way. But there is another and equally important aspect of life on earth."

"What is that?" I asked.

"By the very nature of the human organism", said JFK, "as soon as conditions become just right for it, the most satisfactory amount of food, water, air, and so forth, it begins to decay. As a result, man can survive only when he is opposed by the unremitting hostility of others of his kind, and by various natural enemies. This is the built-in paradox of life on earth, that it faces extinction once it reaches a certain plateau of adjustment to its environment."

"Then man's real enemy is the reformer", I said. "Does that explain the crucifixion of Christ?"

"Not really", said JFK. "Christ's message was not so much a design to make life a physical Paradise, but rather to institute the Kingdom of God on earth. This means that every man would be a king."

"That implies that no man would be a king", I said, "since a king is expected to have subjects."

"It would be the greatest democracy, and the greatest aristocracy of man", said JFK, "because every man would be the king of himself. He would be able to build his life around the divinity within him. This ideal jeopardized the authority of the pluralist groups, and they demanded Christ's crucifixion."

"And we have the same situation today?" I asked.

"Nothing has changed", said JFK. "And perhaps nothing will change, but that doesn't mean that you shouldn't make the effort."

"It sounds simple enough", I said.

"It is simple", said JFK. "You have only to ask man to affirm himself. In this affirmation lies his only hope of saving himself and the earth. Such an affirmation means, of course, the ultimate denial of the pluralist groups."

"But what, if in denying them, man finds it necessary to set up new groups?" I asked. "What if all of this effort only results in a re-grouping of the masses?"

"That still would serve to stave off the catastrophe which threatens mankind", said JFK. "New groups would have to offer mankind some new answers, and all of the old answers of the pluralist groups have been proven to be self-serving and worthless, since they lead man to the edge of the abyss."

"I am willing to do what I can", I said. "You will be available, occasionally, I suppose, to let me know how I'm doing?"

"Certainly not", said JFK. "I've said everything that I have to say. From now on, you're on your own."

The radiance slowly dissolved, leaving me once more alone in the Buick. I looked out the window and saw that the line before John F. Kennedy's grave had gotten much longer. There would be little chance of paying my respects today. Nor was there any chance of passing to the head of the line by announcing that I had a special commitment from him. That might be a beginning, but it would also be the end.

OTHER BOOKS BY EUSTACE MULLINS

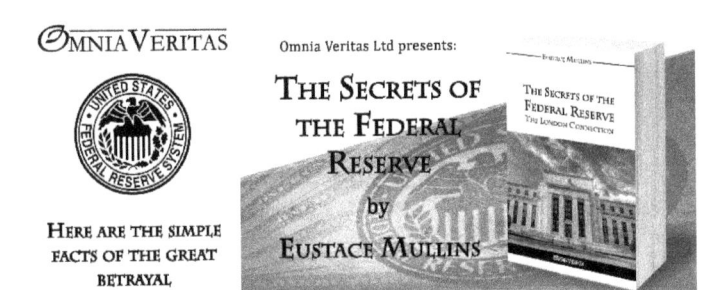

OMNIA VERITAS

Omnia Veritas Ltd presents:

THE SECRETS OF THE FEDERAL RESERVE

by

EUSTACE MULLINS

HERE ARE THE SIMPLE FACTS OF THE GREAT BETRAYAL

Will we continue to be enslaved by the Babylonian debt money system?

OMNIA VERITAS

Omnia Veritas Ltd presents:

THE CURSE OF CANAAN

A demonology of history

by

EUSTACE MULLINS

Liberalism, more popularly known as secular humanism, can be traced in an unbroken line all the way back to the Biblical "Curse of Canaan."

Humanism is the logical result of the demonology of history

OMNIA VERITAS

Omnia Veritas Ltd presents:

THE WORLD ORDER

OUR SECRET RULERS

A Study in the Hegemony of Parasitism

by

EUSTACE MULLINS

The peoples of the world not only will never love Big Brother, but they will soon dispose of him forever.

The program of the World Order remains the same; Divide and Conquer

THE RAPE OF JUSTICE
by EUSTACE MULLINS

AMERICA'S TRIBUNALS EXPOSED

American should know just what is going on in our courts

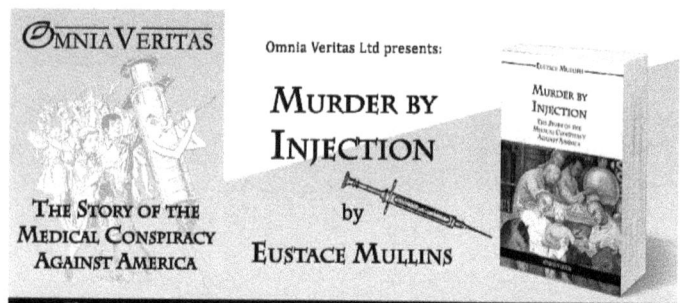

MURDER BY INJECTION
by EUSTACE MULLINS

THE STORY OF THE MEDICAL CONSPIRACY AGAINST AMERICA

The cynicism and malice of these conspirators is something beyond the imagination of most Americans.

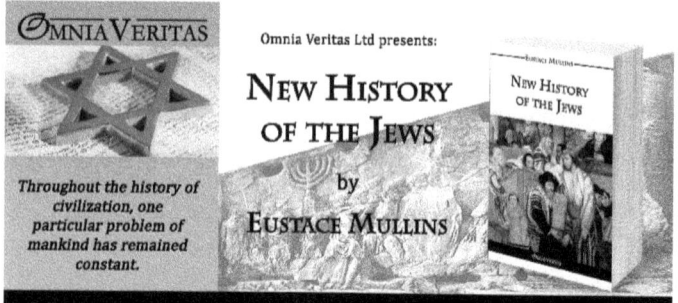

NEW HISTORY OF THE JEWS
by EUSTACE MULLINS

Throughout the history of civilization, one particular problem of mankind has remained constant.

Only one people has irritated its host nations in every part of the civilized world

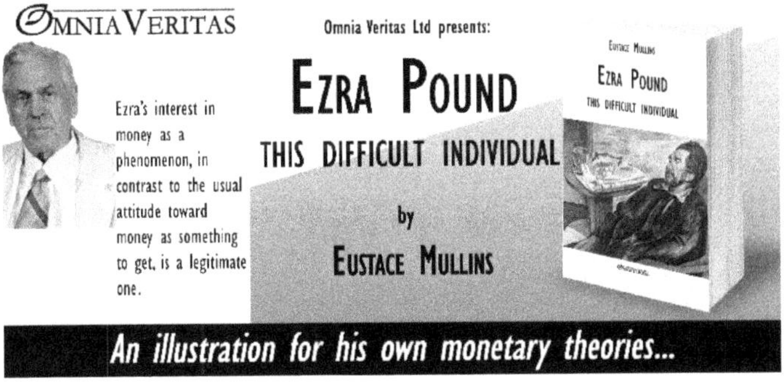

Omnia Veritas Ltd presents:

EZRA POUND
THIS DIFFICULT INDIVIDUAL
by EUSTACE MULLINS

Ezra's interest in money as a phenomenon, in contrast to the usual attitude toward money as something to get, is a legitimate one.

An illustration for his own monetary theories...

MY LIFE IN CHRIST
BY EUSTACE MULLINS

Christ did not wish to be followed by robots and sleepwalkers, He desired man to awaken, and to attain the full use of his earthly powers.

THIS is the story of my life in Christ

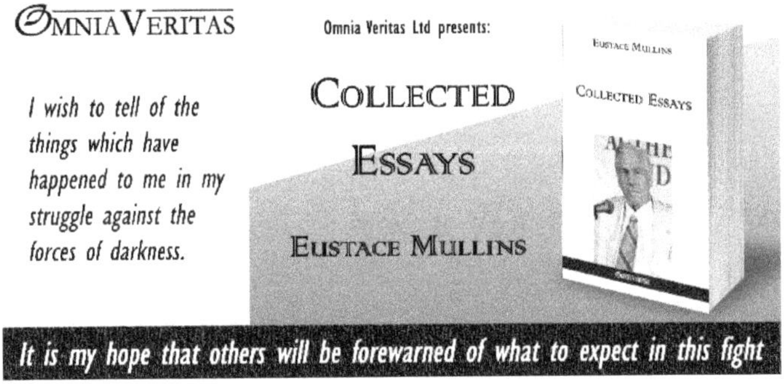

COLLECTED ESSAYS
EUSTACE MULLINS

I wish to tell of the things which have happened to me in my struggle against the forces of darkness.

It is my hope that others will be forewarned of what to expect in this fight

www.omnia-veritas.com

Lightning Source UK Ltd.
Milton Keynes UK
UKHW020320020621
384754UK00011B/2657